THE COLLECTED W

MW01285300

VOLUME III

THE GOD OF
THE BIBLE

JACK COTTRELL

THE CHRISTIAN RESTORATION ASSOCIATION

TABLE OF CONTENTS

PREFACE

I began my first semester of seminary teaching in the fall of 1967. I was teaching five prepared-from-scratch courses, one of which was "The Doctrine of God." Four students signed up for the course. On the first day, one of them asked, "What is the 'doctrine of God' anyway?" I thought to myself, perhaps a bit sarcastically, "This is going to be fun!" And it was! This became one of my signature courses. At first I taught it every year, then toward the end every other year, for my entire 49-year tenure as a seminary professor.

I had taken a course at Westminster Seminary on the doctrine of God, and I had read quite a few books, plus sections in systematic theologies, on the subject. Everything I had absorbed approached the topic in the same way: first, the nature of God; second, the works of God. I came to the conclusion that there is a better way to present the material, namely, to *begin* with the works of God, and then to discuss the aspects of His nature most connected with those works. So that's how I arranged my course: Part One: God the Creator—His work of creation and His nature as expressed therein; Part Two: God the Ruler—His work of providence and His nature as expressed therein; and Part Three: God the Redeemer—His work of redemption and His nature as expressed therein.

In the early 1980s College Press asked me to write the book on God for their "What the Bible Says About" series. I eagerly accepted the task, intending to write a volume called *What the Bible Says About God*. As I wrote, my research expanded to include much more material than I had used when teaching my course. After a while it became clear that I was not going to be able to say everything I wanted to say about God in just one volume. I asked College Press if they would allow me to write *three* volumes on the subject instead, and they graciously agreed. The result was a set of books (now published by Wipf and Stock) called *What the Bible Says About God the Creator* (1983), *What the Bible Says About God the Ruler* (1984), and *What the Bible Says About God the Redeemer* (1987)—about 1,500 pages in all. Then about 25 years later an arrangement was made to condense and update these books into a single volume. The main work of condensation was completed by one of my students, Terry Chaney; and College Press finally got its one-volume work on God: *God Most High: What the Bible Says About God the Creator, Ruler, and Redeemer* (466pp., 2012).

Over the years many occasions arose that called for the preparation of shorter talks and articles about the God of the Bible. Some of those have been collected for this present volume, which I decided to call by the title, *The God of the Bible.* Many of these have been printed before in various venues; for some of them, this is the first time they have been in print. Some of the subjects covered here have been discussed in the books named above, but much of this material is not in those books.

For this present volume I have selected thirty studies, most of which have been produced in the twenty-first century, some as late as 2018. I have reverted here to the traditional way of dividing the material, and have grouped the first seventeen studies around the topic of the *nature* of God, and the next twelve studies around the *works* of God, especially creation and providence.

I will now give some information about how these pieces first came about. Many (about fifteen) of them began as answers to questions submitted to me by inquiring students and ministers and other servants of our Lord. For around ten years I have had a Facebook page, and many questions came to me there. At first I tried to answer them in a feature called "Facebook notes." Then in 2013 someone I did not even know at the time, a fellow Facebooker named Steve Lowman, set up a website for me (www.jackcottrell.com) and transferred all my Facebook notes (up to that time) to that site! As we say down south, *Bless your heart, Brother Steve!* The questions kept coming, and I answered many in short studies on the website.

About that same time, Lee Mason, the head of The Christian Restoration Association (CRA) and the editor of its periodical, *The Restoration Herald*, asked me to write a monthly article for the *Herald* called "Ask the Professor." Over the years many of the studies originally appearing on my website (I'm not sure how many) have also appeared in this monthly column. I won't try to name them here, but you can recognize most of them because they begin with a short paragraph headed, **QUESTION:**.

Three of the studies included here are longer essays that I think are appearing in print for the first time, two of which are quite recent. I prepared these two as oral presentations for special brotherhood meetings. These are the most "theological" of the essays herein, and in many ways the most significant. I hope you will pay special attention to them. One is "YAHWEH Is His Name," which I believe you will find very interesting. The other is "God's Eternal Purpose," which I developed quite recently while studying the first chapters of Paul's letter to the Ephesians. The older one is my summary and review of a theological novel that appeared some years ago called *The Shack*. I include this here because that book has some serious problems about the nature of God.

There is one communion meditation here, which I believe will give you special insight into the nature of God as it relates to the atoning work of Jesus. It is called, "In the Atonement, Did God the Father Suffer Along with the Son?"

I have also included five studies that were originally presented as sermons, mostly at the congregation at which I and my wife Barbara worship and serve, the First Church of Christ in Greendale, IN (near Lawrenceburg). I am pretty sure Greendale was where I first preached, "Do Muslims and Christians Worship the Same God?" I know the next two were preached at Greendale: "Did God Rig the Election?"—which came shortly after Trump's win in 2016; and "Children of God: Romans 8:14-25," preached first for a seniors luncheon at the Spring Hill Church of Christ in Middletown, OH (at Bob Stacy's invitation), and in this present form later at the Greendale church. When you read this sermon you will see why it fits an audience of senior citizens, and why it was appropriate for me to preach it at Greendale the day before my 80th birthday (2018). Last item in the book is a sermon called "Doxology." It's one of my favorites.

Six of these studies have appeared in periodicals as articles. The one called "Conditional Election" was originally presented as part of a panel discussion on "Problem Passages in Ephesians" at a Conference on Evangelism at The Cincinnati Bible Seminary in November 1965, and later published in the Summer 1966 issue of *The Seminary Review*. (I have updated it a bit here.) At the time of the Conference I had just begun my doctoral studies at Princeton, NJ, in preparation for becoming the first Professor of Theology for the fledgling graduate school at CBS. President W. W. Perry wanted me to be on the Conference program so that our alumni could get to know me. They flew me from a New Jersey airport back to Cincinnati, one week after a plane had crashed into a hillside while landing in Cincinnati, killing everyone aboard. That was my first airplane flight.

The essay on "The Predestination of Individuals" comes from the October 4, 1970, issue of the *Christian Standard*. I was replying to an article from an earlier issue of the *Standard*, written by Brother Donald Nash. Nash was defending the view that God never predestined any *individuals* to heaven; He predestined only a *group* (i.e., whoever would choose to become a part of that group). This is a view called "corporate election," and it appears in various places in Restoration Movement writings. It is an effort to avoid the impact of the Calvinist doctrine of predestination. In my article I show that God's predestination IS a predestination of individuals, and I show why this is very different from the Calvinist view.

Another essay that originally appeared in a periodical is "What Is God Doing in the World?" I wrote it at the request of Lee Mason again, and he published it in *The Restoration Herald*. It is a succinct summary of material I usually discuss when talking about the providence of God. The piece on "The Grace of God" appeared as a solicited essay for *Bible Teacher and Leader* in Fall 1971. It is one of my earliest writings on grace; it has the nature of a devotional study (including citations from many hymns).

That's all I have to say by way of introduction to this material. I am already working on the next two volumes; I believe one will be on Calvinism, and the next on baptism. But for now, I commend this present volume to God for His glory, and I pass it along to my readers for their instruction and edification.

JACK COTTRELL
July 14, 2018

PART ONE

THE NATURE
OF GOD

DESCRIBING GOD

QUESTION: How would you describe God?

ANSWER: I appreciate the questioner's wanting me to "describe God," but I must confess that a thorough reply to this question would require an answer that is much too large for a brief piece like this. In the early 1980s I set out to answer this question by writing a book on "What the Bible Says About God." Before I finished, I had three large volumes totaling 1,500 pages. Originally published by College Press, they are still available from Wipf and Stock Publishers: *What the Bible Says About God the Creator*, *What the Bible Says About God the Ruler* (on the subject of providence), and *What the Bible Says About God the Redeemer*. Those three large volumes have now been condensed into one volume: *God Most High: What the Bible Says About God the Creator, Ruler, and Redeemer* (College Press, 2012; 466pp.).

When I wrote my systematic theology, *The Faith Once for All* (College Press) in 2002, I included a shorter answer to the question as chapter 3: "The Nature of the Creator-God" (pp. 67-99). In this chapter I divided twenty-five attributes of God into four main categories, and gave a brief explanation of each one. Here I will explain those four categories, and explain the attributes included in each of them even more briefly.

I. GOD'S NONRELATIONAL ATTRIBUTES.

These explain the essence of God as He exists in Himself. I.e., the expression and meaning of these attributes do not depend upon the existence of created beings and God's interrelationships with them. They are true of God and are understandable apart from any connection with creation.

A. God is SPIRIT.

This means He has life and personhood; He is a living, personal being. Because He is "composed of" spirit, He is also nonmaterial and invisible. See John 4:24.

B. God is SELF-EXISTENT.

This is also called His "aseity." It means that His being is not derived from anything outside of Himself. He is self-sufficient, inherently immortal, indestructible, and independent. See Exodus 3:14; John 5:26; 1 Timothy 6:16.

C. God is ONE.

This includes the unity of simplicity, which means God is not composed of parts and His essence is indivisible. It also includes the unity of singularity, meaning He is the only true God. See Deuteronomy 6:4; 1 Corinthians 8:4.

D. God is THREE.

This is the Trinity: He is three persons who share one essence or substance. This does not mean there are three gods, but three distinct centers of consciousness who are eternally equal in essence and authority. Each person within the Trinity takes on distinct roles in the working out of redemption. See Matthew 28:19; 1 Peter 1:2.

E. God is INFINITE.

This means He is not limited in any of His attributes, contrary to the inherent limitations of created beings. E.g., He is not limited by time and space; His power and knowledge are not limited. The only thing that limits God is His own nature; He cannot do things that are contrary to His nature.

F. **God is ETERNAL.**

This is true in a quantitative sense. He has existed from eternity past and will by nature continue to exist into eternity future. He has no beginning and no end. See Psalms 90:2; 102:25-27. Also, this is true in a qualitative sense. Though He is not completely timeless, His consciousness is not limited by time; He has perfect knowledge of the past and the future. See Isaiah 40-48.

G. **God is RIGHTEOUS.**

This means that God is always true to Himself; all His actions are perfectly consistent with every aspect of His nature. He is self-consistent and faithful to His word. See Psalms 129:4; 145:17.

H. **God is IMMUTABLE.** → *God does Not Change*

This means that God does not and cannot change in His nature, character, and purposes. See Psalms 102:25-27; Malachi 3:6. He does change, however, in His mental states (e.g., emotions) and in His activities, especially in the sense that He genuinely reActs to what goes on within His creation.

II. GOD'S ATTRIBUTES AS SEEN IN HIS RELATIONS WITH CREATURES AS SUCH.

These are attributes that become manifest once God has brought the creation into existence. These are expressed in His relationships with created beings.

A. **God is TRANSCENDENT.** → *Above + beyond*

This means He is distinct from and different from all created beings, both in His very essence and in the way in which He exists. His essence is "beyond" that of any creature, not in a spatial sense but in a metaphysical sense. In Biblical terminology, God is HOLY in an ontological sense. As the only uncreated being, He is set apart or separated from all creatures. See Exodus 15:11; Isaiah 6:3.

B. God is SOVEREIGN.

This means He has absolute lordship over all creation. As Creator He owns all things, and thus has inherent authority and power to do whatever He wishes with His creatures. This does not mean that He causes all things; it means He is in control of everything that takes place. See Psalms 47:2,8; 103:19.

C. God is OMNIPOTENT, or all-powerful.

This is a major aspect of His infinity: His power is unlimited. He can do whatever He chooses, except for things that are inconsistent with His own nature. He is "God Almighty." See Genesis 17:1; Jeremiah 32:17.

D. God is WISE.

Wisdom is the ability to choose the best possible end, and then to choose the best possible means of achieving that end. This applies to God's choices in creation, providence, and redemption. If we believe that God is all-wise in his sovereign control of all things, we will have complete trust in Him. See Romans 8:28; 11:33; 16:27.

E. God is GOOD.

This means that He is the standard of excellence and perfection; that He is always morally good; that He is desirable (Psalms 34:8); and that He is kind and benevolent toward His creatures. See Matthew 5:43-45; 1 Timothy 6:17.

F. God is OMNISCIENT - infinite in His knowledge.

He knows everything there is to know; He knows it perfectly; and He is always conscious of all He knows. He has perfect knowledge of the past, the present, and the future. See 1 John 3:20; Isaiah 46:9-10).

G. God is OMNIPRESENT. → Everywhere

This is what it means to say that He is infinite or unlimited by space. He is not three-dimensional; His infinite being is always present to every point of space at all times. In this metaphysical sense we can never be separated from God's presence. See Psalms 139:7-10.

H. God is **IMMANENT**. — *NEAR*

This means that He is not only present TO every point of space; He is also present WITHIN our space. He is not "outside" our universe (a false understanding of transcendence); He is always with us and near us. See Psalms 34:15; Acts 17:27-28.

I. God is **GLORIOUS**. — *Some Total / All That God is*

This refers to His infinite significance, the totality of His perfections, the fullness of His deity compressed into a single concept. He displays His glory in all His works. See Psalms 19:1; 148:13; Isaiah 6:3.

III. GOD'S ATTRIBUTES AS EXPRESSED IN HIS RELATIONS WITH FREE-WILL CREATURES, not just creation as such.

Here we are thinking of His relationships with human creatures who have and use the gift of free will, apart from our identity as sinners.

A. God is **HOLY**.

This is not His ontological holiness, or separation (apartness) from the creation itself, but His ethical holiness, i.e., His separation (apartness) from everything sinful or morally evil. This is His perfect moral excellence, including His own moral purity and uprightness as well as His absolute opposition to and hatred of all sin. Because God is holy, He demands holiness in His creatures as well. See Job 34:10-12; 1 Peter 1:15-16.

B. God is **LOVING**.

This includes both AGAPE love, or His genuine and infinite care and concern for our well-being; and also His genuine AFFECTION or lovingkindness toward us. We may define his love as His self-giving affection and selfless concern that lead Him to actively seek the happiness and well-being of His image-bearing creatures. See Psalms 119:64; John 3:16; 1 John 4:8. — *God is love*

IV. GOD'S ATTRIBUTES MANIFESTED IN HIS RELATIONS TO SINNERS.

These are attributes known to us especially in the way God responds to sinners. They are basically the outflowing of the two previous attributes: because God is holy, He is jealous and wrathful in the face of sin; because He is love, He is merciful, patient, and gracious toward sinners.

A. God is JEALOUS.

Against the threat of false gods and idols, like a loving husband, God is always zealous to protect the well-being of His people and to preserve our exclusive devotion toward Himself. He is provoked to jealousy when His people go after other gods. See Exodus 20:5; 34:14; 2 Corinthians 11:2.

B. God is WRATHFUL.

Wrath is an essential part of God's nature; it is the way His holiness responds to sin. It is the natural and inevitable and eternal recoil of the all-holy God against all that is unholy. Its result is vengeance and retribution in the form of deserved punishment, ultimately in hell. See Isaiah 63:3-4; Romans 1:18; Hebrews 12:29.

C. God is MERCIFUL.

The God of wrath is also the God of mercy. Mercy is the love of God as directed toward mankind in our sin-caused pain, suffering, need, misery, and distress. It means that God hurts because we hurt. It is his sense of compassion that causes Him to want to deliver us from suffering, apart from any consideration that we may actually have brought it upon ourselves by our own sin. See Romans 11:22; 2 Corinthians 1:3; Ephesians 2:4.

D. God is PATIENT, or longsuffering.

This means that He withholds our deserved punishment in order to give us the opportunity to repent and be spared. He exercises delay and restraint in the execution of His wrath, simply because He loves us. See Exodus 34:6; Isaiah 48:9; 2 Peter 3:9.

E. God is GRACIOUS.

Grace as an attribute of God is the most extreme expression of His love when that love comes face to face with sin. It is His willingness and desire to forgive and to accept the sinner in spite of his sin, and to give the sinner the very opposite of what he deserves. It is His infinite desire to give sinners this gift of forgiveness even though they deserve His wrath and even though it costs Him the cross. See Psalms 103:8-12; Romans 3:24-26.

9/11/19

Lord/God

"YAHWEH IS HIS NAME"
EXODUS 15:3

QUESTION: How many gods really exist?

ANSWER: In researching the names of various deities I came across a book entitled *Encyclopedia of Gods: Over 2,500 Deities of the World* (FActs on File, 1993), by Michael Jordan [no, not that one!]. That list does not claim to be exhaustive. I doubt if anyone can compile a complete and accurate list of all the so-called gods that people have believed in down through the millennia.

The Bible, though, has an accurate and complete number and listing of all the "Gods" who really and truly exist, and that number is ONE! There is only one true and living God, and, to quote Exodus 15:3, "YAHWEH is his name." [I need to explain something here. The Hebrew Old Testament actually uses the divine name YAHWEH over 6,000 times, but most modern English translations substitute the words "the LORD" (with LORD all capitals) for the divine name. In this study I plan to use YAHWEH wherever it appears in the Hebrew.]

Our present task is to understand the significance of this magnificent name of God: YAHWEH. Our beginning point is Moses's encounter with God at the burning bush as described in Exodus 3:1-9 (NASB— except as explained above).

> Now Moses was pasturing the flock of Jethro his father-in-law, the priest of Midian; and he led the flock to the west side of the

wilderness and came to Horeb, the mountain of God. The angel of YAHWEH appeared to him in a blazing fire from the midst of a bush; and he looked, and behold, the bush was burning with fire, yet the bush was not consumed. So Moses said, "I must turn aside now and see this marvelous sight, why the bush is not burned up." When YAHWEH saw that he turned aside to look, God called to him from the midst of the bush and said, "Moses, Moses!" And he said, "Here I am." Then He said, "Do not come near here; remove your sandals from your feet, for the place on which you are standing is holy ground." He said also, "I am the God of your father, the God of Abraham, the God of Isaac, and the God of Jacob." Then Moses hid his face, for he was afraid to look at God.

YAHWEH said, "I have surely seen the affliction of My people who are in Egypt, and have given heed to their cry because of their taskmasters, for I am aware of their sufferings. So I have come down to deliver them from the power of the Egyptians, and to bring them up from that land to a good and spacious land, to a land flowing with milk and honey, to the place of the Canaanite and the Hittite and the Amorite and the Perizzite and the Hivite and the Jebusite. Now, behold, the cry of the sons of Israel has come to Me; furthermore, I have seen the oppression with which the Egyptians are oppressing them."

At this point Moses is no doubt getting very excited, but is wondering — "What does this have to do with me?" This is when God's message gets personal, continuing in Exodus 3:10-12:

"Therefore, come now, and I will send you to Pharaoh, so that you may bring My people, the sons of Israel, out of Egypt." But Moses said to God, "Who am I, that I should go to Pharaoh, and that I should bring the sons of Israel out of Egypt?" And He said, "Certainly I will be with you, and this shall be the sign to you that it is I who have sent you: when you have brought the people out of Egypt, you shall worship God at this mountain."

At this point Moses starts to get a little shaky, and he replies (v. 13), "Behold, I am going to the sons of Israel, and I will say to them, 'The God of your fathers has sent me to you.' Now they may say to me, 'What is His name?' What shall I say to them?"

Here is where all of us, including Moses, might be a bit surprised at God's answer (v. 14) — "God said to Moses, 'I AM WHO I AM'; and He said, 'Thus you shall say to the sons of Israel, "I AM has sent me to you."'" Why would we be surprised at this answer? Because as far as we know, God had never revealed Himself by this name—"I AM"—before this. But then God immediately adds this to His answer (vv. 15-18):

> God, furthermore, said to Moses, "Thus you shall say to the sons of Israel, 'YAHWEH, the God of your fathers, the God of Abraham, the God of Isaac, and the God of Jacob, has sent me to you.' This is My name forever, and this is My memorial-name to all generations. Go and gather the elders of Israel together and say to them, 'YAHWEH, the God of your fathers, the God of Abraham, Isaac and Jacob, has appeared to me, saying, "I am indeed concerned about you and what has been done to you in Egypt. So I said, I will bring you up out of the affliction of Egypt to the land of the Canaanite and the Hittite and the Amorite and the Perizzite and the Hivite and the Jebusite, to a land flowing with milk and honey."' They will pay heed to what you say; and you with the elders of Israel will come to the king of Egypt and you will say to him, 'YAHWEH, the God of the Hebrews, has met with us. So now, please, let us go a three days' journey into the wilderness, that we may sacrifice to YAHWEH our God.' ..."

Later, when Moses and Aaron confronted Pharaoh with this request, the conversation went like this (Exodus 5:1-2) —"Thus says YAHWEH, the God of Israel, 'Let My people go that they may celebrate a feast to Me in the wilderness.'" But Pharaoh said, "Who is YAHWEH that I should obey His voice to let Israel go? I do not know YAHWEH, and besides, I will not let Israel go."

Thus at this point the children of Israel remained in slavery, and the rest of Exodus 5 describes how their circumstances actually became worse, and how Moses understandably complained to God. Then in chapter 6:2-3 comes this very puzzling report: "God spoke further to Moses and said to him, 'I am YAHWEH; and I appeared to Abraham, Isaac, and Jacob, as God Almighty, but by My name, YAHWEH, I did not make Myself known to them.'"

This is said in a very matter-of-fact way, but there is actually a huge problem here. In this statement to Moses, God Himself says, "By My name, YAHWEH, I did not make Myself known to them," i.e., to Abraham, Isaac, and Jacob. The problem is this: the entire book of Genesis uses the name YAHWEH throughout, beginning in 2:4. God obviously identified Himself as YAHWEH to the human race, because the record shows that numerous people spoke of and to God as YAHWEH, e.g., Eve (4:1), Lamech (5:29), Noah (9:26), and ESPECIALLY Abraham, who built an altar to YAHWEH, and called on the name of YAHWEH (12:8), and addresses Him as "YAHWEH God" (15:2). God specifically said to Abraham, "I am YAHWEH who brought you out of Ur of the Chaldeans" (15:7). There is much more of the same, regarding not only Abraham but also Isaac and Jacob.

So what in the world does God mean in Exodus 6:3, when he says, "By My name, YAHWEH, I did not make Myself known to them"? THAT is what I will now explain.

The key is to understand that at this point in history (as Exodus 3 begins to record it), TWO NEW THINGS are happening that are related to each other. The connection between these two new things will explain this strange-sounding statement in Exodus 6:3, and will show why this statement is consistent with the book of Genesis. Remember: TWO NEW THINGS are taking place.

I. FIRST NEW THING: A NEW REVELATION OF THE *MEANING* OF THE NAME OF GOD.

Going back to Exodus 3:14-15, we find that for the very first time, *God is explaining what the name YAHWEH means!* From the beginning of history (see Genesis 2:4) human beings, including Abraham, Isaac, and Jacob, *knew* God by this name and *called* Him by this name; but they did not know what it MEANT! They did not know the significance of it. God never explained it to them. But as I understand it, this is what he is now doing with Moses, as recorded here in Exodus 3:14-15. When Moses asked God what name he should use when people ask him, "Who sent you?", God gave this answer and "said to Moses, 'I AM WHO I AM'; and He said, 'Thus you shall say to the sons of Israel, "I AM has sent me to you."'" He then immediately follows this with this statement: "Thus you shall say to the sons of Israel, 'YAHWEH, the God of your fathers, the God of Abraham, the God of Isaac, and the God of Jacob, has sent me to you.'"

What do we see here? We see God for the first time explaining the meaning of his name, and at the center of this explanation is an important connection between the name "YAHWEH" and the new name "I AM."

The fact is that most scholars accept this connection, but they cannot actually explain how it works. Why not? Because the Hebrew four-consonant word for YAHWEH (yod — hē — vav - hē , represented by YHWH) is rather mysterious! This word has no *clear*, indisputable relationship to other Hebrew or Semitic words.

For one thing, we are not even sure how to *pronounce* it. Some used to say "Jehovah," as in the 1901 American Standard Version of the Bible, and some older hymns ("Guide me, O Thou great Jehovah, pilgrim through this barren land; I am weak, but Thou art mighty, Hold me with Thy powerful hand."). In the more recent gospel song by Twila Paris, "We will glorify the King of Kings," the second verse begins, "Lord Jehovah reigns in majesty, we will bow before His throne." In our times, though, the most-accepted pronunciation is "YAHWEH." But one Old

Testament scholar says this is still an "educated guess" (Terence Fretheim, *New International Dictionary of Old Testament Theology and Exegesis*, Zondervan 1997, IV: 1297).

More importantly, from an etymological perspective, we are not sure what the word *means*. As another Biblical scholar says, "It is impossible to state indisputably what [YHWH] means" (Gottfried Quell, "*kurios*," *Theological Dictionary of the New Testament* [Kittel], Eerdmans 1965, III: 1069).

Our English translations do not help us with either pronunciation or meaning, since most of them substitute for YHWH the English words "the LORD," with "LORD" capitalized. So where can we go to find the meaning of this glorious name? The most obvious place is: right here in Exodus 3!

Scholars seem to agree that, even if they cannot discern *exactly* what it is, there is a definite connection between these TWO statements of God to Moses in reply to Moses's question, What shall I say when they ask me the NAME of the one who sent me? These two statements are: "I AM has sent me," and "YAHWEH has sent me."

"I AM" is simply the Hebrew word for "to be, to exist," and its Hebrew consonants, hē — vāv - hē (represented by HWH), are three of the four consonants in the name YAHWEH. More importantly, it is God Himself who brings these two names together in answer to the one question—what is your NAME? I believe that God is here revealing to Moses (and to all of us) that his name YAHWEH is somehow based on the affirmation, "I AM" — indeed, "I AM WHO I AM." I agree with Quell: "The name of God is meant to express something like existence" (ibid., 1072).

Here is the point: when the God of Abraham, Isaac, and Jacob says YAHWEH "is my name forever" (Exodus 3:15), he is telling us that he alone is the *only true God*, the only one who really and truly EXISTS! His basic attribute is his EXISTENCE, i.e., his "I AMness"! This attribute belongs to no other so-called "gods."

We could spend a lot of time talking about variations of God's "I AMness" or existence. For example, we can point to His *self*-existence, also known as His aseity, which means that He owes His existence to nothing or no one outside Himself. We could mention His *eternal* existence—His eternality or immortality, which means that He has no beginning and no end. We could discuss His *unchanging* existence or immutability, which means that He does not grow, develop, or change.

But the main point God is making here in Exodus 3, and the one I am stressing, is God's UNIQUE existence! This means simply that contrary to all the so-called deities created in the imagination of sinners, YAHWEH is the only God who truly, really, existentially EXISTS.

But now we will raise a very important question: why does God choose this point in time (as described in Exodus 3) to reveal this about His name? Remember that I said above that "at this point in history TWO NEW THINGS are happening that are related to each other"? One of these new things is what we have just explained, i.e., God's new revelation of the meaning of YAHWEH as His "I AMness." We will now explain the OTHER new thing, and show how it is crucially connected to the "I AMness" of God.

II. SECOND NEW THING: GOD'S FIRST GREAT WORK OF REDEMPTION — THE EXODUS.

We need to remember that when God appeared to Moses here at the burning bush (Exodus 3), the Israelites had already been in Egypt for hundreds of years, and for most of that time they were treated as slaves by the Egyptians. At this point in time God determined that it was time for his chosen people to assume the task for which he had chosen them. But to make this happen, God had to DELIVER them from the state of bondage and slavery. In other words, he had to REDEEM them. So what we have here is *God's first great work of redemption—a redemptive* work, a *saving* work! (This is the other *new thing*.)

In Exodus 6:5 God says to Moses, "I have heard the groaning of the sons of Israel, because the Egyptians are holding them in bondage." Then he says (v. 6), "I am YAHWEH, and I will bring you out from under the burdens of the Egyptians, and I will deliver you from their bondage. I will also redeem you with an outstretched arm and with great judgments."

Throughout this great gospel message from God Himself (Exodus 6:2-8) God stresses the fact that His name is YAHWEH: I will do this redemptive work because I am YAHWEH! "I am YAHWEH, and I will bring you out" of Egyptian bondage (v. 6)! "I will take you for My people, and I will be your God; and you shall know that I am YAHWEH your God" (v. 7). "I will bring you to the land which I swore to give to Abraham, Isaac, and Jacob, and I will give it to you for a possession: I am YAHWEH" (v. 8).

Why is it so important for God to connect His name YAHWEH— "I AM"—to this work of redemption? Because in this new redemptive work YAHWEH is about to perform, He is going to demonstrate in ways never before expressed that *He alone is the one and only true and existing God*! He is about to demonstrate that all the so-called "gods" of the Egyptians (and of everyone else) are non-existent, fraudulent phonies!

How is He going to do this? Through the TEN PLAGUES He is about to send upon the land and people of Egypt. These plagues were not necessary just to secure Israel's freedom. The Almighty God could have done this in any number of other less violent and less complicated ways. So why did He choose this way? The main point was to demonstrate the *impotence* and, yea, the *non-existence* of the so-called "gods" served by the Egyptians—and thereby to demonstrate the sole existence of the GREAT I AM—YAHWEH—the God of Israel!

Remember Pharaoh's first reaction to Moses's message: "Thus says YAHWEH … Let my people go" (Exodus 5:1)? Here is Pharaoh's haughty reply (5:2): "Who is YAHWEH that I should obey His voice to let Israel go? I do not know YAHWEH, and besides, I will not let Israel go." Moses is instructed to keep saying to Pharaoh, "Thus says

YAHWEH, the God of the Hebrews, 'Let my people go, that they may serve me!'" (9:13). And then, as if to say, "I'll show you who YAHWEH is!"—God continues: I will send plagues on you, "so that you may know that there is no one like Me in all the earth" (9:14).

This is why God kept hardening Pharaoh's heart so that he would not let the Israelites leave until God had made his point. This is why God hardened his heart even to the point of causing Pharaoh and his army to pursue them to their own destruction in the Red Sea, saying — "And the Egyptians will know that I am YAHWEH" (14:4)

Through these mighty demonstrations of his power God was also impressing on the hearts of the people of *Israel* his "I AMness" — his existence as the one true and living God. How did the Israelites react to their miraculous deliverance through the Red Sea? "When Israel saw the great power which YAHWEH had used against the Egyptians, the people feared YAHWEH, and they believed in YAHWEH and in His servant Moses" (14:31). The result was a glorious psalm of worship and praise, recorded in the first 18 verses of Exodus 15. See verses 1-3 and 11:

> Then Moses and the sons of Israel sang this song to YAHWEH, and said, "I will sing to YAHWEH, for He is highly exalted; the horse and its rider He has hurled into the sea. YAHWEH is my strength and song, and He has become my salvation; this is my God, and I will praise Him; my father's God, and I will extol Him. YAHWEH is a warrior; YAHWEH is His name … . Who is like You among the gods, O YAHWEH? Who is like You, majestic in holiness, awesome in praises, working wonders?"

Throughout the Old Testament, to its very end, the people of Israel knew the one true eternally self-existing God as YAHWEH. The Old Testament ends with a prophecy of "the coming of the great and terrible day of YAHWEH" (Malachi 4:5-6).

III. IF THE NAME "YAHWEH" IS SO IMPORTANT, WHY DO WE NOT USE IT TODAY?

The above discussion raises an important question: if the divine name YAHWEH is so important, why do we not use it today? Indeed, why does the New Testament itself not use this name for God? The switch from Hebrew to Greek language is not a sufficient explanation. So, is there a reason why YAHWEH is not used? Yes, and it is very important—as I will now explain.

As indicated above, in the Exodus account *two new things* happened together. ONE, God revealed something new about his name YAHWEH, namely, that this name *means* "I AM," the *Existing One*. TWO, this was done in connection with a new kind of working of God on earth—the *redemptive* activity of the Exodus. These two new things were closely connected: new redemptive work; new revelation of God.

Now here's the deal: At the beginning of this New Covenant era, the *very same thing* happened again! Just as it happened at the time of the Exodus, the same two kinds of new interrelated realities occurred together: a new redemptive work of God, and a new revelation of WHO GOD IS.

The new redemptive work is the aggregate of the work of Christ and the Holy Spirit: the incarnation of the Logos as Jesus of Nazareth, Jesus's atoning work of the cross, Jesus's resurrection from the dead, Jesus's ascension and enthronement at the right hand of God, and the pouring out of the indwelling presence of the Holy Spirit on the Day of Pentecost. As great as the Exodus miracles were, these new redemptive works of Christ and the Spirit are INFINITELY GREATER — because they accomplish the *redemption of believers from slavery to sin and their freedom to live eternally in fellowship with God.*

But what is just as amazing is that the God who has accomplished this redemption has revealed Himself in connection with it in *magnificently new ways!* What is this new revelation of Himself that God has unveiled to us in connection with this new redemptive work? It is indeed something

NEW—a break-through revelation concerning God's very nature. It is a new knowledge of who God is, a knowledge that is required for us to understand this new redemptive working that he has performed.

The new revelation is this: that God is a TRINITY! God has now revealed to us his *trinitarian* nature — that YAHWEH is not just one person, but is THREE persons! He is ONE GOD, but he has three centers of personhood, three centers of consciousness, three centers of activity. He is three divine persons who are doing *different things,* performing *different tasks* in this new redemptive activity of God. There are hints of his plurality in the Old Testament, but his Threeness is not actually revealed until in this New Covenant era, in connection with his new redemptive works.

What is there about this new redemptive work that involved *dividing up* its phases among the different persons within the Trinity? Primarily, it begins with the fact that only one person of the Trinity became visibly incarnate as a human being and performed the works of atonement and resurrection—the one called God the Son. Then, to top off all of this, another person of the Trinity comes among us spiritually in order to facilitate within believers an inner healing from sin and a power to live holy lives; this is the divine person called God the Holy Spirit. All these distinctive works seem to be coordinated by a third person of the Trinity, the one called God the Father. See 1 Peter 1:1-2, "Peter, an apostle of Jesus Christ, to those who reside as aliens, scattered throughout Pontus, Galatia, Cappadocia, Asia, and Bithynia, who are chosen according to the foreknowledge of God the Father, by the sanctifying work of the Spirit, to obey Jesus Christ and be sprinkled with His blood."

These three distinct divine persons MAY have been doing distinctive works in the pre-Christian era, but it was not necessary for anyone to know about it. What we do know is this: God has *always* existed as Three Persons. These Three Persons always exist as a unity—as One God known as YAHWEH. In Old Testament times God's people knew Him specifically in his ONENESS.

But now, in this New Covenant age, in connection with the new redemptive works of God, we know that YAHWEH is Three Persons, and we now relate to each of these Three Persons *individually*. We do not call Him YAHWEH, the "I AM," "the Existing One" — but we COULD! It would be OK. But for us, God now has a NEW name—the *Trinitarian* name. See Matthew 28:18-19, "And Jesus came up and spoke to them, saying, 'All authority has been given to Me in heaven and on earth. Go therefore and make disciples of all the nations, baptizing them in the name of the Father and the Son and the Holy Spirit ... .'" It is significant that Jesus says "Into **THE NAME**" — the ONE name: *The Father, the Son, & the Holy Spirit.*

The point is that we now know God in his *Threeness*. In many ways we relate to each person equally. E.g., we worship them equally. When we say "God," we are often referring to all three persons in their Oneness. When we sing the "Doxology," for example, we say, "Praise God from whom all blessings flow," referring to the one True and Living God. And then we say, "Praise Father, Son, and Holy Ghost"— distinguishing the Three Persons and giving them equal worship. But much if not most of the time, we relate to each of these Three Persons in distinct ways, in view of their distinct roles in our salvation. For example, we *pray to* the Father. Also, we take the Lord's Supper mainly to honor the Son, for making our *forgiveness* possible. And, we depend on the Holy Spirit's indwelling power for our inner *sanctification*.

There are many, many more ways in which our awareness of the Threeness of God makes our lives very different from the lives of believers in the Old Covenant era. But we cannot ever forget that these Three Divine Persons together are: YAHWEH! God the Father is YAHWEH. God the Son is YAHWEH. God the Holy Spirit is YAHWEH. Each one is YAHWEH — not identically, but equally. And together, they are the One True God, the Existing One, the I AM.

WHO IS YAHWEH (JEHOVAH) IN THE OLD TESTAMENT?

QUESTION: Recently I saw an article that declared that Yahweh (Jehovah) in the Old Testament is God the Father *only*, and that he does not include the other persons of the Trinity. The article specifically said that Yahweh and Christ Jesus are two distinct individuals. Is this Biblical? What do you think?

ANSWER: I saw the same article, and I disagree with the view presented there. I believe that Yahweh as the name for God revealed in the Old Testament includes all three persons of the Trinity. Depending on the context, this name may refer to all three persons or to any one of them. The New Testament makes this very clear regarding the divine nature of Jesus Christ, and based on this I simply infer that it would apply to the Holy Spirit also. Here I will present the New Testament evidence that the Old Testament name "Yahweh" is inclusive of the Logos, i.e., the second person of the Trinity, the one who became Jesus of Nazareth. (See my book, *The Faith Once for All*, Ch. 13, "The Person of Christ," pp. 233-234, 240-241.)

First, we will notice the connection between the name "Yahweh" and the New Testament title for Jesus, i.e., "Lord" (the Greek word *kurios*, or *kyrios*). The title "Lord" is used for Jesus almost 500 times. This is significant because of the way the title *kurios* was used among the Jews. In most extant manuscripts of the Septuagint (the Greek translation of the

Old Testament), *kurios* is the Greek word used around 8,000 times to refer to the God of Israel. Sometimes it translates the Hebrew terms *'adonai* ("Lord" in a literal sense) and *'elohim* ("God"). However—and here is the crucial point—over 6,000 times *kurios* appears in the place of "Yahweh," the divine name itself. In nearly a thousand of these cases, *kurios* appears in combination with *theos*, "God," in the common expression "the LORD God." It is never used for pagan deities and idols.

The bottom line is this: any Jew who knew the Old Testament in its Septuagint form would have associated this title (*kurios*) immediately with the one true God. This is certainly the case with the Apostle Paul and other New Testament writers, who frequently quote from the Septuagint version of the Old Testament.

It is significant, then, that the New Testament writers use this title so frequently—in Paul's case, almost exclusively—for Jesus. There is no way that they could have applied this title to Christ in its religious sense without in their minds identifying Him with Yahweh. This is especially true after His resurrection from the dead, as a result of which Thomas addressed Him as "my Lord [*kurios*] and my God" (John 20:28). God the Father declared Him to be "both Lord and Christ" (Acts 2:36), and the whole world will ultimately "confess that Jesus Christ is Lord" (Philippians 2:11), indeed, the "Lord of lords" (Revelation 17:14; 19:16). The latter is a title used for God (Deuteronomy 10:17; 1 Timothy 6:15), and surely there can be only one "Lord of lords." Thus when the early Christians confessed "Jesus is Lord" (Romans 10:9; 1 Corinthians 12:3), they were confessing belief in His deity and identifying Him with Yahweh.

Second, it is a fact that in a number of instances New Testament writers apply to Jesus Christ specific Old Testament passages that speak unequivocally of Yahweh. For example, Matthew 3:3 says that Isaiah 40:3 is talking of John the Baptist's ministry as the forerunner of the Messiah: "Make ready the way of the LORD, make His paths straight!" But Isaiah 40:3 speaks specifically of Yahweh: "Clear the way for the LORD [Yahweh] in the wilderness; make smooth in the desert a highway for our

God." The same is true of Malachi 3:1, where Yahweh says, "Behold, I am going to send My messenger, and he will clear the way before Me." In Matthew 11:10, however, the Holy Spirit sees fit to change *Me* to *You*, thus showing that the specific reference is to Jesus: "Behold, I send My messenger ahead of You, who will prepare Your way before You."

Other passages are equally insistent that Old Testament references to Yahweh are speaking of Jesus Christ. Hebrews 1:10-12 quotes Psalms 102:25-27 and applies it to our Savior, thus ascribing to Him Yahweh's work of creation and attribute of eternality. Joel 2:32 is especially significant: "And it will come about that whoever calls on the name of the LORD [Yahweh] will be delivered." The New Testament quotes this passage on two occasions and refers it to Christ (Acts 2:21, 36; Romans 10:9, 13). In Isaiah 8:13-15 Yahweh describes Himself as a stumbling stone, and in Isaiah 28:16 he declares that he will lay in Zion a firmly-placed cornerstone. In Romans 8:32-33 Paul quotes from and combines these two texts, and implies that the stumbling stone is Jesus Christ (see also 1 Peter 2:6-8). Similar comparisons can be made between Psalms 68:18 and Ephesians 4:6-8; between Isaiah 45:23 and Philippians 2:10-11 (see Romans 14:11); between Deuteronomy 10:17 and Revelation 17:14, 19:16; between Psalms 34:8 and 1 Peter 2:3; between Isaiah 8:14 and 1 Peter 2:5-8; and between Psalms 24:7-10 and 1 Corinthians 2:8.

After surveying passages such as these and many others, Christopher Kaiser says, "We conclude that Jesus is identified with Yahweh, the God of Israel, in virtually all the strata of the New Testament, early as well as late" (*The Doctrine of God*, Crossway 1982, p. 35).

Third and finally, if Jesus in some sense IS Yahweh, how do we explain the fact that the Old Testament at times distinguishes between Yahweh and the Messiah Jesus (as in Psalms 2:7; Psalms 110:1; and Isaiah 53:6, 10, for example)? Here we will make two points.

For one thing, as indicated above, to say that Jesus is Yahweh does not mean that Jesus *alone* is Yahweh, but that Yahweh of the Old Testament *includes* Jesus, along with the Father and the Spirit. Thus in texts such as these, Yahweh the Father is distinct from Yahweh the Son, with the former speaking of the latter.

In addition, strictly speaking, when we say that Jesus is Yahweh, we are referring specifically to his *divine* nature, the eternally pre-existing Logos who *became* Jesus (John 1:1-14). We are not referring to Jesus the human being as such, who did not even exist until he was supernaturally formed in the womb of the virgin Mary (Luke 1:31-35). Prior to his incarnation as Jesus of Nazareth, the Logos co-existed with the Father and the Holy Spirit under the shared name of Yahweh. From this perspective all three persons of the Trinity could foresee and speak about the yet-to-come Messiah, who would take on the identity of Yahweh by virtue of his union with the Logos. Thus even though in a sense the God-man Jesus is distinct from Yahweh, there is a stronger sense in which he IS Yahweh.

Nancy

THE TRUE GOD AND FALSE GODS

QUESTION: The first of the ten commandments says, "You shall have no other gods before me" (Exodus 20:3, ESV), or "no other gods besides me." Also, God is often called El Elyon or "God Most High." Why is this terminology used if these false gods do not exist? Do these gods exist, with God (Yahweh) just being at the top of a hierarchy of deities? Are the false gods demons? Or are they simply statues that never did anything supernatural?

ANSWER: There is definitely a Biblical basis for equating pagan idols with demons, based on 1 Corinthians 10:19-20, "What do I imply then? That food offered to idols is anything, or that an idol is anything? No, I imply that what pagans sacrifice they offer to demons and not to God. I do not want you to be participants with demons" (ESV). This is simply a matter of Satanic deceit, though, with pagans *thinking* their idols are true deities when in fact they are not. Satan is called "the god of this world" (2 Corinthians 4:4), but he occupies this status only in his own mind. There are no other beings who are true deities. The transcendent Creator-God of the Bible is the only being in the category of "God." He alone is the Creator; everything else is in the category of creature (Romans 1:25). This is why he is called "the LIVING God" (Psalms 42:2; Matthew 16:16; 1 Timothy 4:10). See my book, *What the Bible Says About God the Creator*, chapter 8, "The Living God," for more on this theme.

It is true that pagan deities were usually represented by statues made of wood or stone or precious metals, but the Bible never puts such idols into the category of true deities. The Bible rather mocks all such attempts to identify these lifeless chunks of wood or metal as "gods." Jeremiah 10:14 says, "Every goldsmith is put to shame by his idols, for his images are false, and there is no breath in them" (ESV). These "gods of wood and stone" are "the work of human hands, that neither see, nor hear, nor eat, nor smell" (Deuteronomy 4:28, ESV). "Their idols are like scarecrows in a cucumber field, and they cannot speak; they have to be carried, for they cannot walk. Do not be afraid of them, for they cannot do evil, neither is it in them to do good" (Jeremiah 10:4, ESV).

I believe the language of the first commandment is simply driving home this point, i.e., "Do not try to put any humanly-devised or man-made so-called deity into the same arena with the one-and-only true and living God, Yahweh!" That he is "God Most High" means that he is above ALL things, the "King of kings and Lord of lords." It is a title of exaltation. Such language was never meant to grant the actual existence of any false gods.

The bigger picture about this is shown in Psalms 96:3-5 – "Declare his glory among the nations, his marvelous works among all the peoples! For great is the LORD, and greatly to be praised; he is to be feared above all gods. For all the gods of the peoples are worthless idols, but the LORD made the heavens" (ESV). There is a play on words here: "the *gods* of the peoples" is the common word *'elohim* (literally, "gods"), and the word for "*worthless idols*" is *'elilim*, which literally means NOTHINGS. I.e., the pagans *think* that the objects of their devotion are *'elohim*—gods, when really they are *'elilim*—nothings! They are nobodies; they are nothings; they don't exist at all!

The apostle Paul helps us to understand this in 1 Corinthians 8, where he discusses the significance of eating food offered to idols. Here he says (ESV) that "we know that 'an idol has no real existence,' and that 'there is no God but one.' For although there may be so-called gods in heaven or on earth—as indeed there are many 'gods' and many 'lords'—yet for us there is one God, the Father, from whom are all things and for whom we exist, and one Lord, Jesus Christ, through whom are all things and through whom we exist" (vv. 4-6).

DO MUSLIMS & CHRISTIANS WORSHIP THE SAME GOD?

Islam is the world's second largest religion, with around two billion adherents. This is nearly one-fourth of the world's population. Fifty countries are mostly Muslim. Europe has around 50 million Muslims, and the USA around 7 million. These numbers are increasing rapidly.

But isn't that a good thing? Aren't Muslims a religious people, and isn't Islam similar to Christianity? Don't we both trace our faith back to the Old Testament, to Abraham? Don't Christians and Muslims worship the same God? In 2007 George W. Bush said, "I believe that all the world, whether they be Muslim, Christian, or any other religion, prays to the same God." Catholicism's Second Vatican Council (early 1960s) said, "The Muslims profess the faith of Abraham and worship with us the sole merciful God." A 1994 Catholic catechism repeated, "Together with us Muslims adore the one merciful God." In a 2011 poll, 40% of evangelical Christians said Christians and Muslims worship the same God. Even the Muslims' own holy book, the Q'uran (29:46) says, speaking of Christians, "Our God [ALLAH] and your God is one."

The implication is that Christianity and true Islam are practically brothers; faithful Muslims are religious and God-fearing; thus they must be peace-loving. The implication is that we have nothing to fear from this religion in its true form. Of course there are *radical* Muslims—the jihadists, the terrorists like ISIS. But aren't these just deviant fanatics who have twisted what real Islam believes? Surely, if we are all worshiping the same God, we can "rest in peace" about our future.

If this is what you think, I have two words for you: **WAKE UP!!** The fact is that the Islamic religion practiced by the ISIS terrorists is more true to real Islam than what passes for Islam in our general culture. In reality, there is no religion more opposed to Christianity than Islam, and there is no alliance more determined to suppress Christianity and dominate the world than Islam.

In my youth the single greatest threat to world peace was Communism; the single greatest enemy of Christianity was Communism; the most likely candidate to be the anti-Christ was Communism. Today these roles are all filled by Islam—and not just the jihadists, but the religion as such.

In this essay I cannot go into all the problems of the Muslim religion, nor into all the reasons why it is so dangerous to Christianity and the world. My purpose is simply to explain the *most basic error* that many folks have about Islam, namely, the FALSE idea that Muslims and Christians worship the same God. Only under-informed people from both the Christian and the Muslim sides believe that Allah and Yahweh (the God of the Bible) are the same.

Before going into detail I will summarize my main point. The question is this: WHO IS GOD, and HOW DO WE KNOW? We know who God is only because of *revelation*. He has revealed Himself to human beings from Eden onward. But here is a very important point: He did not reveal *everything* about Himself *all at once*, from the beginning. In Old Testament times God got serious about revealing Himself from the time of Abraham onward (c. 2000 B.C.), and then *really* serious from the time of Moses (c. 1500 B.C.). For the next 1000 or 1100 years (up to Malachi, c. 430 B.C.) God was revealing Himself as YAHWEH, the one true God. This revelation is recorded in the Old Testament. Then came centuries of silence.

Then after about 400 years, God began revealing Himself again, but this time with a HUGE, GIGANTIC SURPRISE! In the first century A.D. **SOMETHING HAPPENED** that forever shows that Allah is a false God and that Islam is a false religion. What happened? JESUS CAME! I will now explain in detail what this means.

I. GOD REVEALED HIMSELF IN OLD TESTAMENT TIMES IN HIS *ONENESS*.

In the Old Testament the main thing God revealed about Himself was His *oneness*. This oneness included two things: Yahweh is the ONE AND ONLY God. Also, in His nature Yahweh is just ONE GOD; he is not a collection of deities, like the individual gods of Olympus.

This ONENESS of God is affirmed often in the Old Testament. In Exodus 20:2-3 the first of the Ten Commandments says, "I am the LORD your God, who brought you out of the land of Egypt, out of the house of slavery. You shall have no other gods before Me." The Jews' "golden text" (Deuteronomy 6:4) says, "Hear, O Israel! The Lord is our God, the Lord is one!" Isaiah 44:6 declares, "Thus says the Lord, the King of Israel and his Redeemer, the Lord of hosts: 'I am the first and I am the last, and there is no God besides Me.'" See also Isaiah 45:5, 18, 22 — "I am the Lord, and there is no other; besides Me there is no God ... . I am the Lord, and there is none else ... . Turn to Me and be saved, all the ends of the earth; for I am God, and there is no other."

This ONENESS of God continued to be emphasized in the New Testament. Mark 12:28-29 records a scribe asking Jesus, "What commandment is the foremost of all?" Jesus answered, "The foremost is, 'HEAR, O ISRAEL! THE LORD OUR GOD IS ONE LORD ... .'" In 1 Timothy 1:17 Paul says, "Now to the King eternal, immortal, invisible, the only God, be honor and glory forever and ever. Amen." James 2:19 says, "You believe that God is one. You do well; the demons also believe, and shudder." See also Romans 3:29-30; Galatians 3:20.

Now, if Islam had been invented in the context of Old Testament revelation only (e.g., in the 7th century B.C. instead of the 7th century A.D.), its deity, Allah, would have sounded much the same as Yahweh. This is because in Muslim thought the main thing about Allah is his *oneness*: "There is no God but Allah."

BUT here's the deal: the Old Testament revelation of God is not the whole picture, since the OLD Testament is *not God's final word!* There is more about God than meets the eye in Old Testament times, simply because God did not choose to reveal *everything* about Himself in those days!

(Here's an illustration—and it is JUST an illustration: I am going to tell you something about myself *now*, that I have never told anyone before—something about *who I am*. Here's the deal: I am actually just ONE of **three identical triplets**. Sometimes you have seen one of me, sometimes another, and at other times the third. One of me is the social JACKIE, seen around the community and in local stores and restaurants. But then there is JACK, the recluse who hides in his home office and just studies and writes. The third "me" is JACQUES; he's the one whom you see at church and who travels around and preaches occasionally. So now you know: there is more to me than you thought, up to now! Remember: this is just an illustration! It leads me to my other point, though it is not exactly parallel to my illustration.)

II. IN NEW TESTAMENT TIMES (BEGINNING WITH JESUS CHRIST) GOD HAS REVEALED HIMSELF IN HIS *THREENESS*.

I.e., though He is just ONE GOD, he is *three distinct persons*: God the Father, God the Son, and God the Holy Spirit. We call this THE TRINITY. (In this essay I do not intend to discuss the concept of the Trinity as such; see my book, *God Most High: What the Bible Says About God*, chapter 20).

Our question here is this: Why did God wait so long to make His threeness known? Simply because there was no need for anyone to know this in Old Testament times. So what changed in the New Testament era? With Jesus, the time came to *work the works of salvation!* In the Old Testament era there were prophecies of the cross and of the resurrection, and of the coming work of the Spirit; but now it is time for this saving work to actually be done! The work of salvation is something only God can do, and it actually involves SEVERAL different works, and these various works are *divided among the distinct persons of the Trinity.*

One person (God the SON, the LOGOS) enters our universe and becomes a human being (Jesus), and He alone goes to the cross and experiences death for our sins. Then three days later He is raised from the dead—with the help of God the FATHER and God the SPIRIT. Forty days later He ascends to the right hand of the Father in the angelic heaven. Then after ten more days, on the Day of Pentecost, the risen, ascended, and enthroned God the Son turns to the third person of the Trinity— God the Spirit—and says, "OK, now it's YOUR TURN! They are waiting for you. I told my followers you would come to them now that I have gone. So it's time for you to place your power upon them. They are already gathered in worship, in the presence of thousands of other Jews. Now, Holy Spirit — do your thing!" What happens next is described in Acts 2.

Thus God reveals His *threeness* to us in connection with the working out of our salvation. This is how we now know, in New Testament times, that God is still ONE, but he is MORE than one: he is also THREE. How to explain this is a mystery we may never penetrate. It has no real parallel in human experience. (One possible illustration: a computer system can have *one server*, with *three PCs* attached. But that's another story.)

Here is the main point: *we can no longer say we believe in the ONE TRUE GOD if we do not also accept him as the three persons of the Trinity!* And Muslims adamantly refuse to accept the idea that God is a Trinity of divine persons. Thus they refuse to believe in the same God that Christians worship. As Christians we are committed to a belief in God as three persons from the very beginning of our Christian lives. Let me ask you: when you became a Christian, into whose name were you baptized? Into the name of "God"? No. Into the name of "Yahweh"? No. Into the name of "Allah"? A thousand times NO! Well, how about—into "the name of the Father, and of the Son, and of the Holy Spirit?" *Absolutely*! You see, in the Great Commission Jesus forever finalized the revelation of the threeness (Trinity) of God when He commanded us to baptize into the *one name* of THE FATHER, THE SON, and THE HOLY SPIRIT (Matthew 28:18-20). This is the Christian's God!

A crucial aspect of this new knowledge of God is *the divine nature of Jesus.* Jesus is God! This is the point of the very title, "Son of God" (see John 5:18; 10:33, 36). Also, Jesus is specifically identified with God in John 1:1, 14 — "In the beginning was the Word, and the Word was with God, and the word WAS GOD ... . And the Word became flesh and dwelt among us." In John 20:28, the apostle Thomas confesses Jesus as "My Lord and my God," and is not rebuked or corrected by Jesus. Colossians 2:9 says, "For in Him all the fullness of Deity dwells in bodily form." In Revelation 5:8-12 (as in John 20:28), Jesus is worshiped. See especially John 5:23, where Jesus says that it is the Father's will "that all will honor the Son even as they honor the Father. He who does not honor the Son does not honor the Father who sent Him." To refuse to worship Jesus the Son is to also refuse to worship the Father.

Once the church began, the main reason why so many Jews (who believed in Yahweh as they knew Him from Old Testament revelation) were rejected by God was this: they refused to accept the new revelation of the threeness of God and of the divine nature of Jesus! (See Romans 11:20.) As long as Muslims likewise refuse to accept this revelation, they cannot claim to be worshiping the true God.

Here is the #1 reason why Islam is not a TRUE religion, and why it is nothing like Christianity. The "god" Muslims worship is not the true God! "Allah" is not the God of the Bible—Yahweh, the one true God who is Father, Son, and Holy Spirit. Indeed, the "Allah" whom Muslims worship does not exist. Those committed to Islam, like so many Jews in the church age, have closed their minds and hearts to the true God. They have specifically and vehemently rejected God as Trinity: as Father, Son, and Holy Spirit. They adamantly reject the sonship and the divine nature of Jesus—and thus the salvation He brings. Jesus either IS or IS NOT the Son of God who is God in the flesh. Jesus either IS or IS NOT the eternal God in the human person of Jesus. Jesus either IS or IS NOT one of the three persons of the divine Trinity. The Muslim religion says he IS NOT, and thus unambiguously separates itself from the true God.

III. WHAT LESSONS CAN WE LEARN FROM THIS?

First, we must not hesitate to speak the truth, which includes exposing all false doctrines and false religions, including Islam. In Acts 20:28-31 the Apostle Paul gives this admonition to the elders at the church in Ephesus: "Be on guard for yourselves and for all the flock, among which the Holy Spirit has made you overseers, to shepherd the church of God which He purchased with His own blood. I know that after my departure savage wolves will come in among you, not sparing the flock; and from among your own selves men will arise, speaking perverse things, to draw away the disciples after them. Therefore be on the alert … ." In Ephesians 4:14 Paul warns us to be on guard against being "tossed here and there by waves and carried about by every wind of doctrine, by the trickery of men, by craftiness in deceitful scheming." In Titus 1:9 he says that a church leader must be "holding fast the faithful word which is in accordance with the teaching, so that he will be able both to exhort in sound doctrine and to refute those who contradict."

Second, we must realize that just because Islam is a religion, this does not mean it is a TRUE religion. Just because it affirms belief in "one god," this does not mean that their god is the one TRUE God. Just because many Muslims say (perhaps sincerely) that they want to live in peace with Christianity, this does not mean that true Islam, rightly understood, is a friend of Christianity. I can guarantee all of you who are non-Muslims that you do not want to live in a world, or a country, run by Muslims and governed by Islamic law. Christianity in our time has no greater enemy on earth than Islam.

Third, the fact remains that Jesus said: LOVE YOUR ENEMIES! (Matthew 5:44). So we must love Muslims, and recognize that without their acceptance of the true God, they are lost for eternity. And if we love them, we will want them to know this. And finally, if we love them, we will try to lead them to the knowledge of the true God and to the knowledge of salvation in Jesus Christ.

WHAT IS THE TRINITY?

QUESTION: I have a relative who is a Jehovah's Witness. He accepts that Jesus is the son of God but denies that he (Jesus) is God. How would you explain the triune God?

ANSWER: For details, see chapter 3 of my book, "What the Bible Says About God the Redeemer" (pp. 117-174). This entire chapter is an explanation of the Trinity. In this brief answer I will summarize how I explain the Trinity in my book, "The Faith Once for All" (pp. 70-73).

We begin with the obvious: God is ONE, but He is also THREE. He is one and three at the same time. This is the doctrine of the Trinity. There is no Biblical *term* that actually means "trinity." For example, this is not the connotation of the KJV word "Godhead" nor of the Greek terms which it represents. We do find the *concept* of the Trinity in Scripture, however.

Exactly what is this concept? The classical Christian doctrine is usually summed up thus, that God is three *persons* who share one *essence* or substance. A "person" is a thinking, willing center of consciousness. That God is THREE persons means that within the one divine nature are three individual centers of consciousness. Each of the persons is fully conscious of Himself as distinct from the other two and as existing in eternal interpersonal relationship with the other two. We call these three persons the Father, the Son, and the Holy Spirit.

Though they are three, these persons are nevertheless one God. Whatever the concept of the Trinity means, it does not mean that the essence of God is somehow divided into three distinct units. Also, whatever the concept of the Trinity means, it does not mean that there are three separate Gods; this would be tritheism.

Within the context of the Trinity, that God is ONE means that the three centers of consciousness share one and the same divine essence or being or substance. This is not just saying that they share the same *kind* of essence (which they do), but that they also share the same specific essence. To say that Father, Son, and Spirit are one in essence means that the totality of divine substance, the whole of "whatever it is to be God," belongs to each of them. The main implication of this is that each is equally divine. In whatever sense the Father is divine, so also are the Son and the Holy Spirit divine. All the attributes of divinity belong equally to each of the three. It cannot be otherwise, since they share the *same essence.*

Upon what is the doctrine of the Trinity based? It is derived only from the special revelation of the Bible, and generally not from the Old Testament but from the New Testament. The Old Testament has some hints of the Trinity, but only in the New Testament does the doctrine of the Trinity become an inescapable conclusion.

The one specific fact that makes it impossible for us to avoid the doctrine of the Trinity is the New Testament teaching about the deity of Christ. If Scripture did not portray Jesus as both distinct from the Father and yet as Himself God in the flesh, the question of the Trinity may never have arisen. The same is true to a lesser extent of the Bible's portrayal of the Holy Spirit as a divine person.

In addition to the teaching about the deity of Jesus and of the Spirit are several passages linking the three persons together in a formula-like way that emphasizes their essential equality. The baptismal formula in Matthew 28:19 is the most well known and most influential of these: "Go therefore and make disciples of all the nations, baptizing them in the name of the Father and the Son and the Holy Spirit." Another is the benediction in 2 Corinthians 13:14, "The grace of the Lord Jesus Christ, and the love of God, and the fellowship of the Holy Spirit, be with you all." See also 1

Corinthians 12:4-6 and 1 Peter 1:2. All of these passages show that Christians are redemptively related not just to an abstract deity but to the three persons who are the one true and living God.

Other trinitarian texts are Romans 15:30; 1 Corinthians 6:11; 2 Corinthians 1:20-21; Galatians 4:6; Ephesians 2:18; 3:14-17; 5:18-20; 1 Thessalonians 5:18-19; 2 Thessalonians 2:13; Titus 2:13; 1 John 4:13-14; Jude 20-21; Revelation 1:4-5.

Is God's threeness something that manifests itself as He relates to the world, or is it a real aspect of God-in-Himself? Actually it is both, as Christians have long affirmed. It is mainly seen, though, in the various relationships and works of the different persons of the Trinity toward the world. For example, God the Father foreknows and chooses (Romans 8:29; 1 Peter 1:1-2). The Father also sends the Son and the Spirit; he is never the one sent (John 5:37; 14:26; 20:21). On the other hand, only God the Son became incarnate, lived among us as a human being, died on the cross, was raised from the dead, and is seated at the right hand of the Father as our only High Priest and mediator. In turn, God the Spirit is responsible for regenerating and sanctifying work (1 Peter 1:1-2), beginning on the day of Pentecost (Acts 2:38). He also is the agent of inspiration (2 Peter 1:21), including speaking in tongues (Acts 2:4).

But in addition to the distinct redemptive works through which the three divine persons relate themselves to the world, the threeness of God also exists in the divine essence in and of itself totally apart from such relationships. This is called the ontological Trinity. This intra-divine threeness is the basis for satisfying and loving relationships among the three persons from and for all eternity.

We must be on guard against heretical denials of the doctrine of the Trinity. Some deny the oneness of God and affirm polytheism. This is common among pagan religions, and is true of Mormonism and the original Armstrongism. Others deny the threeness of God, saying there is only one truly divine person. An example is fourth-century Arianism, which taught that Jesus is not truly God but is a created being. Jehovah's Witnesses are modern-day Arians. Another denial of God's threeness is any form of unitarianism, which says there is only one divine person.

One kind of unitarianism is called modalism, which says that in His inner nature there are no distinctions within God. Only in His external relations with His creatures does God *assume* different modes or roles in order to make Himself known and accomplish His purposes among men. These modes are successive, not simultaneous. E.g., In Old Testament times the one divine person revealed Himself as Father; then He became incarnate as the Son; now He relates to his creatures as the Spirit. A modern example of modalism is the "Oneness movement" among certain Pentecostal bodies, also known as the "Jesus only" Pentecostals.

The doctrine of the Trinity is filled with mystery. That God is one and three at the same time is beyond our ability to understand completely. We should never think of it as being absurd or contradictory, however. That would be true only if we think that God is one and three *in the same numerical sense*. But this is not the case. He is ONE in one sense, i.e., one essence; and He is THREE in another sense, i.e., three persons.

IS GOD MORE THAN THREE PERSONS?

QUESTION: We speak about the "three persons in the Godhead," i.e., the Trinity. We also say that God has *revealed* Himself in these three persons as performing different roles for salvation purposes. Is it not possible that the omnipotent God could reveal Himself in MORE than three persons with other roles? Perhaps he has revealed Himself in just three persons because these are enough and sufficient to save mankind.

ANSWER: This speculation is quite faulty, and it is based on a false assumption that there is some connection between the *persons* of the Trinity and the ways in which God *reveals* Himself. This is the false assumption that underlies the Trinitarian heresy called "modalism," which says that the three *persons* of the Trinity are nothing more than three different ways or "modes" in which He reveals Himself. I.e., sometimes He reveals Himself as Father, sometimes as Son, and sometimes as the Holy Spirit. He is always one and the same *person*, however (according to this view).

This approach to God, and specifically to the Trinity, is contrary to Scripture and is seriously false. It is actually a form of unitarianism. See my books, *What the Bible Says About God the Redeemer* (College Press), 140-146; and *The Faith Once for All* (College Press), pp. 73, 253-255.

It is true that God can reveal Himself in many different ways or modes (Numbers 12:6-8; Hebrews 1:1-2). Sometimes He reveals Himself through His deeds or acts, which are manifested as supernatural events in our history (e.g., the ten plagues upon Egypt). Sometimes He reveals

Himself through His words, either spoken by Himself (e.g., the Ten Commandments, Exodus 20:1-19) or spoken through His prophets (e.g., Moses, Deuteronomy 18:15-19). Sometimes He reveals Himself through visible forms of various kinds (human shapes, as Genesis 18:1ff.; animal shapes, as Luke 3:21-22; shapes of objects, as Exodus 13:21-22). Once He has revealed Himself as an actual human being, when He became incarnate in the person of Jesus of Nazareth (John 1:1, 14). [Caution: the Logos did not become incarnate simply as a means of revealing God to us; He came to work the works of redemption. But in His incarnate presence among us, He could not help but "show us the Father" (John 14:8-11).]

When God reveals Himself in visible forms (the third type of revelation in the previous paragraph), this is called a *theophany*, literally, an appearance or manifestation of God. The form that He takes can be anything He chooses. He simply brings that visible entity into being (probably via creation *ex nihilo*), and it remains in existence only for the time required for the revelation, after which it disappears back into nothingness.

Any one of the three persons of the Trinity can become manifest in this way for revelation purposes; and there is no limit to how many such manifestations are possible over time or at any one time. For example, in the angelic (invisible) universe, in which there is a divine throne room, (probably) God the Father manifests Himself to the angels in a permanent spiritual theophany, making Himself visible to the angels at all times (e.g., Revelation 4 and 5). After the Judgment Day He will *also* make Himself visible to saved human beings in a permanent physical theophany on the New Earth (Revelation 21:3; 22:1-5). These two theophanies will be eternally simultaneous.

We should never think that these theophanies, either in their form or content, are somehow the very essence of God. We should not assume that God has these or any other shapes, nor should we assume that the essence of God's being is substantive and spatial in the way that created entities are. When the saints of old saw these theophanies, they were not seeing the pure divine essence. When we shall see the theophanies in the angelic throne room and on the New Earth, we shall not be seeing the pure divine essence. Paul tells us decisively that God "dwells in unapproachable light, whom no one has ever seen or can see" (1 Timothy 6:16). Those who have seen and/or will see God (e.g., Matthew 5:8) are seeing only a manifestation of God brought into being for revelation purposes, and not his true and pure essence.

The main point here is this. With few exceptions (such as the incarnation), the various ways or modes in which God has revealed and can reveal Himself to us *have no inherent connection with the persons of the Trinity as such.* When we speak of the three persons of the *economic* Trinity as dividing up the works of redemption, these are the WORKS of God and are not directly related to ways in which God reveals or manifests Himself to us.

Based on the revelation we have in the Old Testament and New Testament, we must conclude that God exists as one divine being or essence, in three (and only three) distinct persons. Though God's plurality was known in the Old Testament era, His divine threeness was then hidden. It is definitely brought to light in the New Testament writings, however. The New Testament is clear and emphatic about this threeness (e.g., Matthew 28:19; 1 Corinthians 12:4-6; 2 Corinthians 13:14); to posit anything beyond this threeness is unwarranted and useless speculation. [If there is any significance to the number seven in "the seven spirits who are before his throne" in Revelation 1:4; 3:1; 4:4; 5:6, we simply do not know what it is.]

IS MODALISM A SERIOUS HERESY?

QUESTION: I have a question about modalism. I know the early church condemned it as a heresy, but is it serious enough to be a threat to one's salvation? What is the Biblical evidence against it?

ANSWER: Traditional, orthodox Christian faith says Jesus Christ is not only equal with the Father; He is also distinct from the Father in that He is a separate, distinct person, i.e., a separate center of consciousness with His own distinct thoughts, emotions, and actions. This point seems more than obvious to most Christians; but occasionally, in a misguided effort to explain the Trinity, some have embraced a seriously false view called modalism. From its earliest known forms in the late second century, modalism seems to have been a serious attempt to account for God's threeness while emphasizing his oneness. Thus it may be called a particular view of the Trinity, albeit a heretical one. O. J. Brown (*Heresies*, Doubleday 1984, p. 99) says that this is "the most common theological error among people who think themselves orthodox," mainly because "it is the simplest way to explain the Trinity while preserving the oneness of God." But as Brown says, "Unfortunately, it is incorrect."

Modalism is basically the view that in His inner nature there are no distinctions within God, threefold or otherwise. However, in His external relationships with His creatures, God assumes different modes in which to make Himself known and accomplish His purposes among men. In its original form the contention was that in the Old Testament era God revealed Himself as Father; then He became incarnate as the Son; finally, after Jesus' ascension, God relates to His creatures as the Holy Spirit. Thus these modes of relationship are successive, not simultaneous. It should be noted that viewing the Trinity this way allows one to say that Jesus as God the Son was fully divine, and that the Holy Spirit is also divine. The problem is that the Father, Son, and Spirit are not really distinguished from one another. In their true being they are one and the same person, a person who assumes different modes in His outward relationships to His creatures. God the Father *is* God the Son, who also *is* God the Holy Spirit.

The best known early modalist was Sabellius in the early third century; thus the view is sometimes called Sabellianism. In more recent times varying versions of this view are found mainly in modernistic religion, but also in certain conservative circles such as Oneness Pentecostalism. Modalism also appears from time to time within the Restoration Movement.

All forms of modalism must be rejected as seriously false doctrine. This view simply cannot do hermeneutical justice to the many, many passages of Scripture which speak of Father, Son, and Spirit as being together, not only alongside each other but interacting with one another. Sometimes all three persons are described as being together, and sometimes just two of them; but the implication is the same: the relationship or interaction is real and not just a charade. Luke 1:35 is an example: "The angel answered and said to her, 'The Holy Spirit will come upon you, and the power of the Most High will overshadow you; and for that reason the holy Child shall be called the Son of God.'" The most natural explanation is that both the Father (Most High) and the Spirit were involved in the incarnation of the Son. Another example is the baptism of Christ, where Father, Son, and Spirit are described as simultaneously being involved in different ways: "And the Holy Spirit descended upon Him in bodily form like a dove, and a voice came out of heaven, 'You are My beloved Son, in You I am well-pleased'" (Luke 3:22). Here the Father speaks to the Son in direct address. If this is not one person speaking to another, then the narrative or even the act itself is deceptive. The same applies to the many occasions when Jesus addressed the Father in prayer (e.g., Luke 22:42; 23:34; John 11:41-42; 17:1-26). Jesus' teaching concerning the coming of the Holy Spirit in John 14-16 is a welter of double-talk if Father, Son, and Spirit are not distinct. For example, Jesus said, "I will ask the Father, and He will give you another Helper" (John 14:16; see also John 14:26; 15:26). The same applies to the record of the fulfillment of this promise in Acts 2; see especially 2:33.

Many other passages are robbed of their natural meaning by modalistic presuppositions. The following examples will suffice: "Therefore, when He comes into the world, He says, … 'Behold, I have come … to do Your will, O God'" (Hebrews 10:5, 7). "I will surely tell of the decree of the LORD: He said to Me, 'You are My Son, today I have begotten You'" (Psalms 2:7). "The LORD says to my Lord: 'Sit at My right hand, until I make Your enemies a footstool for Your feet'" (Psalms 110:1). "But of that day or hour no one knows, not even the angels in heaven, nor the Son, but the Father alone" (Mark 13:32). "And the Word was with God" (John 1:1). "For God so loved the world, that He gave His only begotten Son" (John 3:16). "God has sent forth the Spirit of His Son into our hearts" (Galatians 4:6). "I also overcame and sat down with My Father on His throne" (Revelation 3:21). "Salvation to our God who sits on the throne, and to the Lamb" (Revelation 7:10).

Many other passages could be cited, but these are enough to show that Father, Son and Spirit are distinct persons who exist simultaneously and interact with one another.

H. O. J. Brown points out that modalism not only leaves us with hermeneutical chaos, but also raises serious doubts about the reality of the works of redemption themselves. "Logically," he says, "modalism makes the events of redemptive history a kind of charade. Not being a distinct person, the Son cannot really represent us to the Father" (99). Brown is thinking of the reality of the substitutionary atonement, where the Father "made Him who knew no sin to be sin on our behalf" (2 Corinthians 5:21), where God set Jesus forth publicly "as a propitiation" (Romans 3:24-25;

see also Isaiah 53:6, 10). He is thinking of the reality of Christ's role as a mediator between us and the Father (1 Timothy 2:5-6), as our intercessor with the Father (Hebrews 7:25; see 1 John 2:1). Brown is surely correct: these vital works of redemption lose all their meaning in a modalistic view of Christ's relation to the Father.

Above I called this a "seriously false doctrine," and indeed it is. This raises the question of whether someone who believes this false view can be saved. In my judgment the answer is yes, since it does not include a denial of the divine nature of Jesus (as in Arianism, e.g.). The implications of the view are serious enough, though, that anyone who holds it should not be accepted as a teacher, leader, or officer in the church.

(Most of the above is taken from my book, *The Faith Once for All* [College Press], 254-255. More detail is given in my book, *What the Bible Says About God the Redeemer* [College Press; now Wipf and Stock], 141ff.)

IN THE ATONEMENT, DID GOD THE FATHER SUFFER ALONG WITH THE SON?

QUESTION: We talk a lot about how *Jesus* suffered to accomplish atonement for our sins, but did not God the *Father* also share in this suffering? If Christ's suffering was separation from the Father (Matthew 27:46 — "My God, my God, why have you forsaken me?"), did the Father not also experience the grief of this separation, this broken relationship? Thus it seems that not only did Christ pay for our sins, but so did the Father also.

ANSWER: This question rightly assumes that it is possible for God to suffer—something that has often been denied throughout Christian history. Traditional (classical) theism has typically affirmed the "impassibility" of God, a word related to our term "passion," which comes from the Latin *passus*, a participle of the verb *patior*, which means "to experience, to suffer." To say that God is impassible means that He cannot experience emotions of any kind, and especially that He cannot experience sorrow, suffering, or pain. (See my book, *What the Bible Says About God the Redeemer*, 509-511.)

I am glad to say that many have questioned and denied such an idea, and the Bible certainly does not support it. The heart of God is deeply grieved because of sin. This is seen in Genesis 6:6, which says that prior to the flood, "The LORD was sorry that He had made man on the earth, and He was grieved in His heart." The prophets also spoke of this divine suffering, resulting from Israel's rebellion: "But they rebelled and grieved His Holy Spirit" (Isaiah 63:10). In Jeremiah 31:20 God declares, "Is Ephraim My dear son? … I certainly still remember him; therefore My heart yearns for him." The last part of this statement literally says "My bowels are greatly troubled for him," which was a Hebraism for "My heart is filled with agony and mourning." This is how the Old Testament writers used the same expression for their own inward pain; see Psalms 38:8; 42:5; 43:5; Isaiah 16:11; Jeremiah 4:19; 48:36. Thus Jeremiah 31:20 must be applying to God this same condition of the heart. "What kind of condition? The pain! The pain of God!" (Kazoh Kitamori, *Theology of the Pain of God*, John Knox Press 1965, 152-153). For more on this, see *God the Redeemer*, 511-514.

The primary example of divine suffering was the substitutionary death of the incarnate Logos, God the Son. This divine suffering took two forms. First, the divine nature of Christ Himself suffered when He took our sins and our penalty upon Himself on the cross. The incarnate Christ indeed had two natures, divine and human; but He was *only one person*, one center of consciousness. Whatever experiences passed through the consciousness of Jesus of Nazareth thus also passed through the consciousness of God the Son. When Jesus experienced suffering and death on the cross, God the Son experienced suffering and death. "Although He was a Son, He learned obedience from the things which He suffered" (Hebrews 5:8). A particularly poignant aspect of this suffering was "the pain of his God-forsakenness" (Matthew 27:46), as Hendrikus Berkhof put it (*Christian Faith*, Eerdmans 1979, 141). In its full reality, though, God the Son suffered the full equivalent of eternity in hell for the whole human race. Only through this unimaginable agony could He truly be the actual substitutionary atonement for all mankind.

This takes us to the main point raised by the questioner. There was indeed another form of divine suffering connected with the cross, i.e., the suffering of God the Father, the real pain He endured in sending His own Son to die on the cross. This is how Romans 8:32 puts it: "He … did not spare His own Son, but delivered Him up for us all." His own Son! What could be more heart-wrenching than this? One point must be made clear, though. In reference to the cross, the Father did not suffer *what* the Son suffered, but *because* the Son suffered. The Father was not experiencing the agonies of Calvary; only God the Son was experiencing those. The Father rather was experiencing the agonies *of a Father* as he watched His only begotten and only beloved Son go through an ordeal unlike anything eternity had ever seen or will ever see again.

Here is where I believe the questioner goes off the track. ONLY the suffering of Jesus paid for our sins. His role as the incarnate Redeemer was unique among the persons of the Trinity. He alone "bore our sins in his body on the tree" (1 Peter 2:24); He alone became a curse for us (Galatians 3:13); He alone was sent by the Father to be a propitiation for our sins (Romans 3:25; 1 John 2:2; 4:10). The essence of His suffering was much more than a broken relationship with the Father; the separation reflected in Matthew 27:46 was not the essence of the propitiatory suffering, but was the result of it. The essence of the suffering was to be vicariously identified as a sinner and to be enveloped completely within the infinite wrath of the Father.

Thus we cannot assume that if "God" suffers on the cross, then both God the Father and God the Son must be sharing the exact same suffering. If this were so, then Christ's role as Mediator would be compromised. But the Father and the Son do not suffer the same thing. The Son suffers the infinite wrath of the Father upon sin, and the Father suffers to see His Son having to endure it. An analogy would be a convicted criminal being punished by life in prison, and the father of the criminal grieving over his son's fate.

In other words, the suffering of the Mediator is still unique. The basis for making this distinction between how the Son suffers and how the Father suffers is the concept of the economic Trinity. This is the idea that with regard to the works of God, the different persons of the Trinity perform different works and different functions in their relationships with human beings, especially in the outworking of redemption. (See *God the Redeemer*, 159-161.)

We conclude, then, that the doctrine of divine impassibility itself must be rejected because it cuts the very nerve of the gospel of redemption. Kitamori is at least looking in the right direction when he says that the pain of God is "the heart of the gospel," that "in the gospel the final word is the *pain of God*" (19, 47). The only way for God to be true to both sides of His nature—His love and His wrath—is through the suffering of God the Son for the propitiation of the sins of the world. Thus the very nature of the atonement as thus understood *requires* that God suffer as He did in the person of God the Son, in the divine nature of Jesus Christ. Only if Jesus suffered in His divine nature could his substitutionary suffering be *infinite* and thus equivalent to eternity in hell for the whole human race. God's ability to suffer is thus the very presupposition of the atonement. (See *God the Redeemer*, 515-516.)

But at the same time we recognize that this redemptive substitutionary atonement *requires* that an unimaginable suffering likewise be experienced by God the Father, in that He is the one who poured out this wrath upon His own Son. Even though the Father's suffering (like that of Jesus) was made necessary by the need to provide salvation for us sinners, it was nevertheless different from the *kind* of suffering experienced by our Savior Jesus. Only the latter paid the penalty for our sins and set us free from eternity in hell. The Father did not suffer what the Son suffered, just as the Son did not suffer what the Father suffered.

GOD IN THE OLD TESTAMENT AND GOD IN THE NEW TESTAMENT: WHY ARE THEY SO DIFFERENT?

QUESTION: It seems that in the Old Testament God tends to be more legalistic and harsh, while the New Testament is more about the coming of Christ and the gospel of God's love and grace. How do we explain this difference between the two? I know that the same God is acting in both testaments, but why this difference?

ANSWER: Those who take a liberal view of the Bible, i.e., that it is simply the uninspired writings of pious men, assume that over the centuries the idea of God simply evolved from a more primitive and wrathful deity to a more sophisticated and kind deity. We reject this interpretation completely. The God depicted in the Bible from beginning to end is the one true and only God, and His nature and actions in the two testaments are quite consistent. I will make three main points to show you why this is the case.

ONE. One of the most important truths about God (one that is often missed) is that there are two distinct sides to his moral nature. They are summed up succinctly in Romans 11:22, "Behold then the kindness and severity of God" (NASB, ESV). The NIV says "kindness and sternness"; others say "goodness and severity." The Greek word for kindness or goodness means an attitude of goodwill and generosity toward others and a desire for their happiness and salvation. The word for sternness or severity stands for an attitude of relentless commitment to justice, including retributive justice, and a strict upholding of the requirements of the law.

These two sides of God's nature can be summed up in the attributes of LOVE and HOLINESS. I have explained them in detail in my book, *What the Bible Says About God the Redeemer*. Chapter 5 is about "The Holiness of God" (which includes his wrath), and chapter 6 is about "The Love of God" (which includes his mercy and grace).

The point is that *both* of these attributes or character traits exist side by side within God's nature. They are indeed very different and even opposite to one another in some ways, but they are not contradictory; and each is expressed appropriately when the circumstances require it. God would prefer to express the kind and loving side of his nature at all times, but his righteousness requires that the harsher side of his nature be expressed in some cases. It is important to see that the difference is not arbitrary, but is determined by the circumstances within His creation to which He is responding.

TWO. The second main point is that the two covenants and two covenant peoples are NOT PARALLEL to one another. The New Covenant era does not succeed the Old Covenant era like the second half of a football game succeeds the first half. The church does not simply replace Israel as "God's special people," as if they are playing a similar role under their respective covenants. No, the purpose for each is different; and the way God relates to each is different.

Regarding Israel under the Old Covenant, their main purpose was to prepare for the first coming of the Messiah, the man who would be God incarnate, the one who would perform the redemptive works through which "all the families of the earth will be blessed" (Genesis 12:3b). Israel was chosen to be God's instrument for bringing Christ into the world. Everything God did for them and through them was leading up to this goal (Romans 9:4-5). It is a huge mistake to think that Israel was meant to be God's spiritual family within which every individual was promised the gift of salvation. This is the erroneous idea that Paul is refuting in Romans 9-11. Here Paul explains that Israel was chosen for service, not for salvation. Salvation was available to all Jews through God's special revelation, but it was not guaranteed and few (a remnant) actually accepted it. Most of the "chosen people" were actually unbelievers and idolaters, not very different from their pagan neighbors. They were a physical nation, not a spiritual family. It is no wonder that the main side of God's nature displayed in the Old Covenant era was His holy sternness and wrath.

Israel served its purpose, though. It brought the Messiah into the world, and Jesus the Messiah accomplished His purpose through His mighty Acts of redemption, on the basis of which the new people of God, the church, was established. There is a continuity with the *spiritual* Israel of the OT era (Romans 9:6; 11:17ff.), but the new people is of a different kind. It is indeed the KINGDOM of Christ, but not an earthly kingdom (John 18:36). It is a *spiritual* family composed equally of believing Jews and believing Gentiles; this is the "eternal purpose" of God (Ephesians 3:11) accomplished through Jesus Christ. (This is the main point Paul is making in the letter to the Ephesians.) A main purpose of this spiritual kingdom and spiritual family is to spread the saving message of the gospel into the whole world (Matthew 28:18-20)—something Old Testament Israel was never commanded to do. It is no wonder that the main side of God's nature displayed in this New Covenant era is his mercy and grace.

THREE. This leads to my third point, which relates specifically to the difference in the WAYS in which God interacted and interActs with His people in the two different covenant eras. A huge amount of detail could be presented, but I can only summarize it here. The main idea is that in the Old Testament era God interacted with his people (and their neighboring nations) mostly on the physical level, while in this New Testament era God interActs with his people mostly on the spiritual level.

On the one hand, Israel was a physical nation with a physical homeland earned by physical warfare. Membership within the nation was by physical birth, and the sign of membership was physical circumcision.

Her worship was mostly physical. The nation had a physical king, and her history was mainly interaction with other physical nations, who were mainly her physical enemies. Her punishments by God were physical, usually involving these physical enemies (the captivities); and even her spectacular salvation experiences were mainly physical (Exodus from Egypt; return from Babylon). Given Israel's long history (two millennia), the impiety of its people, and the prominence of physical, international events, it is easy to see why the harsher side of God's nature is in the forefront in the Old Testament era.

The New Covenant people of God is indeed a Kingdom, but a *new kind* of kingdom with a new kind of King. His Kingdom is spiritual in nature; or as Luke 17:21 says, it is "within you" (the better translation). God deals with us (the church) in a way totally different from the way He dealt with Israel. Everything is (for the most part) on the level of the spirit rather than the physical. We are all believers, and members of a spiritual family of God based on spiritual birth. Our worship is defined spiritually (e.g., spiritual homeland, Philippians 3:20; spiritual temple, 1 Peter 2:5; spiritual Jerusalem, Hebrews 12:22; worship "in spirit and in truth," John 4:24). Our enemies are spiritual (Ephesians 6:12), and our deliverance is spiritual (the indwelling Holy Spirit, 1 John 4:4). These are all marvelous gifts and a marvelous display of the wonderful grace of God.

I believe this helps explain the picture we get of God in the Old Testament, as contrasted with the picture we get of Him in the New Testament. Without doubt He is the same God, but in the Old Testament era, because of the nature and purpose of the *people* He was dealing with (the physical nation of Israel), and the *way* in which He was dealing with them, the holy (harsh, wrathful) side of His nature is expressed more. In the New Testament era (and remember, the New Testament period of history is less than 100 years) we see the other side of God's nature displayed more prominently, because the nature of the new Kingdom is different, and the way God deals with us is different.

DID MOSES ACTUALLY SEE GOD?

QUESTION: Did Moses actually *see God*, as Exodus 33:18 – 34:8 seems to suggest? How is this consistent with John 1:18, which says, "No one has seen God at any time"?

ANSWER: One attribute of God is that he is *invisible*. One way to understand this is the fact that "God is spirit" (John 4:24), and spiritual essence of all kinds (human, angelic, divine) is naturally invisible to mortal, material eyes. We cannot see even our own spirits, much less God's divine essence.

It is true, though, that God has sometimes chosen to make his presence known among men by inhabiting a specially-prepared material entity that human eyes *can* see. This phenomenon is called a *theophany*, a word from the Greek meaning "an appearance of God." Sometimes this theophany was a human form (e.g., Genesis 3:8; 18:1), and sometimes not (Exodus 13:21-22; Luke 3:22). Many people saw these visible forms, but these forms should not be identified or equated with the pure essence of God.

God is invisible not just because he is spirit, however. This attribute of the divine nature is also the result of the fact that God's essence is uncreated and transcendent. I.e., as uncreated being God is radically different from all created stuff, even the created substance from which angelic bodies are made, and from which our own spirits are made. God's essence is thus invisible to all created beings, including angels, and including ourselves when we shall be in the presence of God in his heavenly glory.

But, do not angels exist in the presence of God now, and do they not *see* Him? Will we not see Him some day (Matthew 5:8; Revelation 21:3)? My answer is no, we created beings—angelic and human— have never seen and never will see the pure, uncreated essence of God. What the angels see is a permanent spiritual *theophany* in which God makes Himself visible to anyone in the angelic world. God has claimed a part of the angelic universe as His visible throne room, where angels can constantly see Him (in His theophanic form), seated on a throne in majestic glory.

On rare occasions some human beings have been allowed the privilege of seeing into the angelic world and into the throne room of God therein; thus they have briefly seen this permanent, constant spiritual theophany that angels see all the time. See Exodus 24:9-11; Isaiah 6:1-5; Revelation 4:2-3.

One of the greatest blessings of our ultimate heavenly home—the new earth—is the fact that God will dwell among us in a glorious theophany similar to the one with which he blesses the angelic world even now. See Revelation 21 and 22. But it will indeed be a *theophany*, not the pure essence of God. Why? Because God is invisible by nature to created beings.

I will now summarize the Biblical teaching about this inherent invisibility of God. The most important passage is 1 Timothy 6:16, which says that God "alone possesses immortality and dwells in unapproachable light, whom no man has seen or can see." This last point is crucial: no man CAN see God. This is not just because God does not LET us see Him; it is because it is inherently impossible. Paul also describes God as "the King eternal, immortal, invisible, the only God" (1 Timothy 1:17); and as "the invisible God" (Colossians 1:15). Romans 1:20 speaks of "His invisible attributes." No man *has seen* God (John 1:18; 5:37; 1 John 4:12); all events suggesting otherwise should be regarded as theophanies.

So where does this leave us with Moses, and the narrative in Exodus 33:18 – 34:8? This episode began when Moses spoke this audacious prayer to God: "I pray You, show me Your glory!" (33:18). Now, Moses had already seen theophanies of God (Numbers 12:8), even in the form of the heavenly presence (Exodus 24:1-11). So what could be the point of Moses's prayer here on this occasion? It is reasonable to assume that he is now asking for something more, i.e., he asking to see God not just in a theophany, not even the glorious spiritual theophany of heaven itself. He is asking to see the very divine essence of God in his pure glory.

This is why God says it is impossible: "You cannot see My face, for no man can see Me and live!" (33:20). In this case "face" means "presence"; i.e., you cannot see the divine presence itself. But even though Moses's prayer cannot be answered in the way Moses is hoping, God does grant him what is apparently a one-of-a-kind experience. He says to Moses, I will place you in a crevice in the rock and cover it with my hand; then I will allow My glory to pass by the crevice. Then I will take away my hand—"and you shall see My back, but My face shall not be seen" (33:21-23). It is generally agreed that "My back" refers not to a bodily part of God (since he does not have a literal body), but to the after-effects or the residue or the wake left by the passing-by of God's unapproachable glory. This is not the same as a direct viewing of the essence of God in Himself (which is impossible anyway), but it is no doubt as close as any creature has come to seeing the actual being of God.

The remarkable thing about this whole episode is that God would choose to answer such a presumptuous prayer at all! It is in this context that God made this theologically pregnant statement: "I Myself will make all My goodness pass before you, and will proclaim the name of the LORD before you; and I will be gracious to whom I will be gracious, and will show compassion on whom I will show compassion" (33:18-19). Calvinists try to interpret the latter part of this statement as a prooftext for unconditional election, i.e., God's choosing whom he will save and whom he will reject. The context shows, however, that God's gracious and compassionate choice here is not about salvation at all, but about God's sovereign prerogative in answering prayer.

In other words, God's references here to grace and compassion are not about soteriological (saving) grace, but about his sovereignty in deciding whom he will bless and whom he will not bless, or what prayers he will answer and what prayers he will not answer. As we saw, Moses has put some strong pressure on God to grant a presumptuous request. So God is replying, in effect, "All right, I will do what you ask, though it is highly unusual. And I want you to know that I am not doing this just because you have won an argument with me or have backed me into a corner. I am granting your request because I want to. I still decide what prayers I will answer and whom I will bless."

See my discussion of God's invisibility in my book, *What the Bible Says About God the Creator* (1983), 222-233; and my discussion of God's conversation with Moses in *What the Bible Says About God the Redeemer* (1986), 362-365.

THE RIGHTEOUSNESS OF GOD

In Christian circles, the Biblical expression "the righteousness of God" has often been the focal point of discussion and controversy. For example, Martin Luther testifies that his deliverance from Roman Catholicism came when he began to understand this phrase in Romans 1:17 as God's gift of righteousness to unrighteous sinners, rather than as a term describing the character of God. Thus in a real sense, this discovery triggered the Reformation and continues to symbolize the difference between the Catholic and Protestant views of salvation.

I believe Luther was correct in understanding "the righteousness of God" in this way in Romans 1:17 (and in other passages, such as Romans 3:21, 10:3; Philippians 3:9). Still, in most cases the term *does* refer to an attribute or aspect of God's nature.

But now the question is, what is the meaning of this divine attribute? Exactly what do we mean when we say God is righteous or just? This question is a matter of serious dispute today, and the stakes in the dispute are quite high.

The most common traditional view is that righteousness or justice (the terms are interchangeable in Scripture) refers to the side of God's nature which requires that He treat people exactly as they deserve, no more and no less. Since all have sinned and deserve only punishment, our only experience of God's righteousness is in the form of wrath and retribution. This is then seen in contrast with the other side of God's nature (i.e., His love, which causes Him to be merciful and gracious even toward sinners and thus to seek their salvation).

In our time, however, many are repudiating this view and are defending a new understanding of God's justice. The tendency is to interpret God's righteousness basically as His faithfulness to His covenant relationships with His people, the main emphasis being not on the demands of His laws but on the keeping of His promises.

Thus the main expression of divine justice is His activity that saves and delivers His people from bondage and oppression. It is an almost altogether positive concept, with the ideas of wrath and punishment being practically excluded. It is equated variously with mercy, love, or grace; or else it is seen as an expression of one of these. It involves wrath or punishment only to the extent that such might be necessary to express fully the divine grace.

What is at stake in this dispute? No less than the nature of ethics and the nature of redemption itself. Regarding the former, it is obvious that justice is a key ethical concept (e.g., criminal justice, civil justice, social justice). Now, Christians usually agree that justice on the human level is rightly patterned after God's justice.

What are the implications of this according to the traditional view, wherein divine righteousness means treating people as they deserve and especially pouring out retribution and wrath on sinners?

Among other things, it means that law and order will be emphasized, usually as the responsibility of human government. It means that emphasis will be placed on protecting the innocent (e.g., via police officers and via armed forces that may justly engage in defensive warfare) and punishing the guilty (e.g., via penal systems that are retributive and not just rehabilitative, and via capital punishment) with impartiality.

But under the influence of the new understanding, where justice is understood as nothing more than a form of love and grace, retributive justice fades out of sight, and the main emphasis falls on "social justice," usually in the form of defending the oppressed and meeting the needs of the poor.

Thus, justice is no longer seen as giving a person what he *deserves*, but giving him what he *needs*. Impartiality gives way to partiality toward the poor. Economic justice becomes a primary concern, usually in the form of attacks on capitalism and a defense of socialism. The church as well as the government must see the pursuit of such justice as their primary task.

This thinking underlies the old social gospel, contemporary liberation theology, and most left-wing evangelical ethics. An example of this last is Stephen Mott's *Biblical Ethics and Social Change* (Oxford, 1982).

Regarding the nature of redemption, the traditional understanding of God's justice sees sin as a violation of His holy nature and the sinner as the object of His wrath. The cross then is understood as propitiation, with Christ as our substitute who turns the divine wrath away from us by taking it upon Himself. Thus God saves us without compromising His justice (Romans 3:26).

But when the revisionists all but equate justice with love, the retributive elements of wrath and punishment are no longer a factor in our redemption. This leads to a rejection of the substitutionary nature of the atonement. Christ's death becomes no more than an act of covenant faithfulness or a moral influence upon us to repent. An example is the writings of Robert Brinsmead, such as in *The Christian Verdict* (Essays 6-8, 1983).

What is the correct view of the righteousness of God? In my book, *What the Bible Says About God the Redeemer* (College Press, 1987), I have attempted to show that neither is correct, because God's righteousness cannot be exclusively identified with just one side of His nature—neither His holiness nor His love.

The concept of righteousness is more general than this. Basically, it means "conformity to a norm." Since God's own nature is the only norm to which He must conform, to say that God is righteous means simply that all His actions are perfectly consistent with His nature.

Thus, God will always be true to His nature. Since God is both holy (which includes wrath toward sin, Hebrews 12:29) and loving (which includes grace toward sinners, 1 John 4:8), that He is righteous means that He will always be true *both* to His holiness (including His wrath) *and* to His love.

This means that the traditional view of ethics and of the atonement are correct, since God's righteousness does include an element of retribution (though it should not be limited to this). Likewise, the revisionist approaches to social ethics and the atonement, which depend on a concept of justice identified almost solely with love and mercy, are false.

(The full documentation and exegetical basis for the above are in *God the Redeemer*, chapter 4, pp. 175-243.)

HOW CAN A GOD OF LOVE BE A JEALOUS GOD?

QUESTION: If God is love, why does He say He is a jealous God?

ANSWER: One of the biggest mistakes made in reference to God's nature is to assume that LOVE is His primary attribute, the one over-arching, all-inclusive attribute that must somehow include all other attributes. This false presupposition seems to underlie this question, i.e., isn't jealousy somehow inconsistent with love? How can love express itself in jealousy?

One of my main theses with reference to God is that there is no ONE, over-arching attribute of which everything else must be an expression. With reference to His moral attributes, there are TWO main and co-equal attributes that are very different but not inconsistent (see Romans 11:22). These two basic sides of His moral nature are His *holiness* and His *love*. Because God is holy, He is jealous and wrathful in the presence of sin; because He is love, He is merciful, patient, and gracious toward sinners. His jealousy is thus an expression of His holiness, not His love.

Here I will explain the attribute of jealousy by providing an excerpt from my book, *The Faith Once for All* (College Press, 2002), pp. 93-94. (See my book, *What the Bible Says About God the Creator* [College Press, 1983], pp. 409-416, for a more complete explanation.)

The holiness of God when provoked by sin sometimes springs forth in the form of *jealousy*. In the second commandment Yahweh declares, "For I, the LORD your God, am a jealous God" (Exodus 20:5). "You shall not worship any other god, for the LORD, whose name is Jealous, is a jealous God" (Exodus 34:14).

Both the Old Testament and the New Testament words for jealousy refer to an intense feeling of zeal or ardor, a fervor of spirit, a zealousness, a jealousy, even a jealous anger. But we must not think of God's jealousy as a petty spite or envy directed toward some other deity whose legitimate worshipers He covets. Rather, when jealousy is attributed to God, the background always seems to be His relationship with His people understood figuratively as a marriage relationship. Like a husband, God is jealous with a "godly jealousy" (2 Corinthians 11:2) for both the welfare of His spouse and for the maintenance of her exclusive devotion toward Himself. And what is the major threat to both? Idolatry! Thus the biblical references to God as a jealous God most often appear in a context condemning idolatry. This connection is seen in Exodus 20:5 and Exodus 34:14, cited above. See also Deuteronomy 6:14-15, "You shall not follow other gods, any of the gods of the peoples who surround you, for the LORD your God … is a jealous God" (see Deuteronomy 4:22-24; 29:17-20). In Deuteronomy 32:21 the Lord declares, "They have made Me jealous with what is not God; they have provoked Me to anger with their idols." See Joshua 24:19-20; Psalms 78:58; 1 Corinthians 10:22.

False gods provoke God to jealousy because they are rivals to His exclusive claim to Godhood and to His exclusive right to the devotion of His creatures. This is where the concept of the marriage relationship enters. Those who are led astray by false gods are being unfaithful to their rightful spouse; idol worshipers are guilty of spiritual adultery or harlotry. See Numbers 25:1-2; Jeremiah 5:7; Ezekiel 16:17; 23:25-27. Just as any husband would be hurt and indignant because of his wife's unfaithfulness, the holy God is provoked to jealousy when His people go after other gods. The heart of this attribute is seen in Isaiah 42:8, "I am the LORD, that is my name; I will not give my glory to another, nor my praise to graven images." As the only true God, he declares, "I will be jealous for My holy name" (Ezekiel 39:25).

From these many passages, it is quite easy to see that God takes idolatry personally; He is injured and insulted by all futile attempts to rob Him of His exclusive position as deity and His exclusive claim to worship. Thus we can see that His jealousy is obviously an expression of His holy wrath. But let us not separate it altogether from love. The equation of idolatry to spiritual adultery should not merely call up the image of a jealous husband who is selfishly filled with anger toward his unfaithful wife. In addition to that, if not more so, it shows us that God is filled with loving concern for His creatures who are spurning His rich grace and are pursuing false hopes while losing everything. He is unselfishly jealous for the well-being of those whom He loves and for whose benefit He has sacrificed His only begotten Son. In this way we can see that His jealousy is actually an expression of His love as well as of His holiness.

THE GRACE OF GOD

The doctrine of grace lies at the very heart not merely of all Christian theology but also of all Christian experience. If we have an incorrect or inadequate understanding of the biblical teaching on grace, our whole grasp of the meaning and purpose of Christianity will be deficient in consequence. There is, accordingly, no subject which is more vital for our study and comprehension than this subject of the grace of God. (Philip E. Hughes, But for the Grace of God [Westminster 1964], p. 9)

This declaration by Hughes is definitely true. But many will say, "I already know what grace is. It is the unmerited favor of God." This, too, is correct. But it is one thing to be able to quote a correct definition, and quite another thing to be overwhelmed by a personal understanding and experience of grace.

Our purpose here is to explain the meaning of the grace of God so that it may be more meaningful to us personally. We shall see that God's grace is three things: His attitude toward us, His action for us, and His action in us.

Grace first of all is God's attitude toward us. Because God is love, He looks upon His creatures with an attitude of favor and good will. When the good will of God considers creatures who are in misery and need, it is characterized as mercy. When His good will considers creatures who are sinful and unworthy and unlovely, it is called grace. Thus grace is the free and undeserved favor of God toward us sinners, who have neither claim upon it nor compensation to render for it.

When we say that grace is the *undeserved* favor of God, we are emphasizing the fact that *sinners* are the object of God's love. We have sinned and turned against God, but He loves us anyway. Though we are against Him, He is still for us; He is on our side! The songwriter marvels that "Christ receiveth sinful men." But that is just what grace is! "*Sinners Jesus will receive; sound this word of grace to all*"!

Grace as undeserved favor is the opposite of justice. If God were to treat us according to justice or law, then He would give us what we deserve. And as sinners, we deserve eternal punishment. But we are saved by grace. That is, God does not treat us as we ought to be treated. We are unworthy of the love He has for us. This is why grace is "amazing"—that God would save "a wretch like me"! This is the wonder of it:

> *I know not why God's wondrous grace*
> *to me He hath made known;*
> *Nor why, unworthy, Christ in love*
> *redeemed me for His own.*

That grace is undeserved favor means that there is no "ought" in grace. We cannot say that God *ought* to be gracious to us. This is a contradiction of terms.

> *For nothing good have I whereby*
> *Thy grace to claim.*
> *I'll wash my garments white*
> *in the blood of Calvary's Lamb.*

God's grace is not only undeserved; it is also free. This means that no compensation is required for it; it is a gift. "But if it is by grace, it is no longer on the basis of works: otherwise grace is no longer grace" (Romans 11:6). Our works are not required as compensation for God's grace. They are our way of thanking Him for the grace freely given.

Just as no compensation is required for grace, so also is no compensation allowed for it. Let us not insult God by trying to "do enough to make up for" His gifts of grace. Let us realize that God accepts us "just as we are, without one plea." May we truly say –

Nothing in my hand I bring;
simply to Thy cross I cling.
Naked, come to Thee for dress.
Helpless, look to Thee for grace.

Grace, then, as God's attitude toward us, is His free and undeserved love to us as sinners. To stand in the grace of God (Romans 5:2) means to acknowledge and to appropriate and to enjoy this favor and love.

But the grace of God is not just a passive attitude or an abstract attribute of His nature. His grace is active. His gracious attitude is demonstrated in gracious action: action for us and in us.

Everything that God has done *for* us in order to accomplish our salvation is grace in action. That eternal counsel wherein salvation was planned was a counsel of grace. It was "to the praise of the glory of His grace" that He chose us in Christ before the foundation of the world (Ephesians 1:4-6).

That God chose the Jewish nation in order to prepare for the coming Savior was not due to any special qualifications on Israel's part. God elected them by grace for His own purpose (Deuteronomy 7:6ff.; 9:4). The fact that God endured their rebellion and unbelief century after century can be explained only by His gracious desire to save sinners.

The most concrete embodiment of the grace of God, however, is Jesus our Lord. The law came through Moses, but "grace and truth were realized through Jesus Christ" (John 1:17). God's grace was "freely bestowed on us in the Beloved" (Ephesians 1:6). He has showed "surpassing riches of His grace in kindness toward us in Christ Jesus" (Ephesians 2:7). "For the grace of God has appeared, bringing salvation to all men" (Titus 2:11).

Jesus Christ Himself is Immanuel, God-With-Us. How is God with us in Jesus? Certainly in that He is among us, incarnate in the flesh. But Jesus Christ is also the certain proof that God is *with* us and not *against* us. We are sinners; we are against God. Rightfully God should be against us. Yet here is the wonder of grace. When God comes among us, He comes not as destroyer, but as Savior. Could there be a clearer demonstration of grace?

> *Oh, the love that drew salvation's plan;*
> *oh, the grace that brought it down to man!*
> *Oh, the mighty gulf that God did span – at Calvary!*

The words of this hymn remind us that of all that God did for us, it is the cross that reveals grace in its sharpest focus. "Mercy there was great and grace was free." Where? "At Calvary"! Here it was that God took the One who knew no sin, and made Him to be sin for us (2 Corinthians 5:21). He suffered the penalty for *our* sins, that we might escape that penalty and be saved.

> *Was it for crimes that I have done He groaned upon that tree?*
> *Amazing pity! Grace unknown! And love beyond degree!*

May we never think of Calvary without thinking of grace, the free and undeserved favor of God which substituted the sinless Christ for us sinful creatures.

> *Marvelous grace of our loving Lord,*
> *grace that exceeds our sin and our guilt,*
> *Yonder on Calvary's mount outpoured,*
> *there where the blood of the Lamb was spilt.*
> *Sin and despair like the sea waves cold,*
> *threaten the soul with infinite loss;*
> *Grace that is greater, yes, grace untold,*
> *points to the Refuge, the mighty Cross.*

Finally, in thinking of those things that God has done *for* us that demonstrate His grace, we cannot forget the gift of His written word, the Bible, which makes known to us the whole wonderful story of His grace.

The grace of God is His attitude toward us that is demonstrated in His gracious action for us. But the activity of grace does not stop with the saving work of God in the life and work of Christ. To those who respond to that grace, God gives more grace. He works graciously *in* the life of the believer who submits to His power. "For by grace you have been saved through faith" (Ephesians 2:8). By grace he has called us through His word out of darkness into His marvelous light. We are "loved with everlasting love, led by grace that love to know." The songwriter testifies that it is "by Thy call of mercy, by Thy grace divine" that "we are on the Lord's side."

By grace God forgives us, counting us righteous because of Christ even though we are sinners, covering our sins with the righteousness of Christ. We are "justified as a gift by His grace through the redemption which is in Christ Jesus" (Romans 3:24). In Christ "we have redemption through His blood, the forgiveness of our trespasses, according to the riches of His grace" (Ephesians 1:7). "Wonderful grace of Jesus, greater than all my sin!" "Plenteous grace in Thee is found, grace to cover all my sin."

By grace God leads us in paths of righteousness, giving us the power and ability to do His will (Philippians 2:13). "As sin reigned in death, even so grace would reign through righteousness to eternal life through Jesus Christ our Lord" (Romans 5:21). This shows that it is grace working in us that gives us the power to overcome sin. The hymn says, "I need Thy presence every passing hour. What but Thy grace can foil the tempter's power?" What gives us strength? "Through days of preparation, Thy grace has made us strong"!

The work of grace fills us with Christian graces, enriching us and equipping us for service. "Therefore … let us have grace, by which we may serve God acceptably with reverence and godly fear" (Hebrews 12:28, NKJV). "We have gifts that differ according to the grace given to us"

(Romans 12:6). Paul often spoke of his ministry as a gift of grace (e.g., 1 Corinthians 15:10, "But by the grace of God I am what I am"). So we, too, can say, "Consecrate me now to Thy service, Lord, by the power of grace divine."

Of all the Christian graces that are bestowed upon us by God's grace, it is meekness or humility that is most consistent with the very character of grace. To know we are saved by grace teaches us humility, according to Ephesians 2:8-9: "For by grace you have been saved through faith; and that not of yourselves, it is the gift of God; not as a result of works, so that no one may boast." Humility is recognizing our emptiness before God, the unworthiness of even our best works. Even our righteousnesses (not just our sins!) are as filthy rages before God, as Isaiah 64:6 says. Let us not be like the Pharisee in Christ's parable, when he thought that his good works qualified him for good standing with God. It was the humble tax collector, who knew his worthlessness and confessed it to God, that was forgiven and accepted by God (Luke 18:9-14).

> *Naught have I gotten but what I received;*
> *grace hath bestowed it since I believed.*
> *Boasting excluded, pride I abase;*
> *I'm only a sinner saved by grace!*

Also, it is grace that upholds us in times of trial. Concerning Paul's thorn in the flesh, the Lord said, "My grace is sufficient for you" (2 Corinthians 12:9). "When darkness veils his lovely face, I rest on His unchanging grace." He "gives me grace for every trial."

Then when we finally reach our heavenly destiny, it will have been because "grace hath brought us safe thus far, and grace shall lead us home." It is "by the gift of His infinite grace" that we are "accorded in heaven a place." "Therefore, prepare your minds for action, keep sober in spirit, fix your hope completely on the grace to be brought to you at the revelation of Jesus Christ" (1 Peter 1:13). And until we get to that heavenly place, it is grace that fills our hearts with joy on the way. "Looking to Him for the grace freely promised, happy, how happy, our journey above."

When we consider all these ways in which the free grace of God is poured out upon us unworthy creatures, we must say, "Oh, to grace how great a debtor daily I'm constrained to be"! We cry out, "Come, thou fount of every blessing, tune my heart to sing Thy grace"!

Oh, for a thousand tongues to sing
my great Redeemer's praise,
The glories of my God and King,
the triumphs of His grace.

We call upon all to "sing the wondrous love of Jesus, sing His mercy and His grace"! "Hail Him who saves you by His grace, and crown Him Lord of all"!

DOES GOD "HATE SIN AND LOVE THE SINNER"?

QUESTION: We have all heard the saying, "God hates the sin but loves the sinner." But is that true? Would it be fair to say, at least as far as the unbeliever is concerned, that God both loves the sinner *and* hates the sinner?

ANSWER: That God hates the sin but loves the sinner is true, but it is not the whole truth.

A. H. Strong (*Systematic Theology* [Judson, 1907], 290) rightly observes that God both hates and loves the sinner at the same time—"hates him as he is a living and willful antagonist of truth and holiness, loves him as he is a creature capable of good and ruined by his transgression." In other words, God does hate the sin, and He also hates the sinner.

The Bible clearly teaches that God's hatred is directed against the *person* who sins and not just the sin itself. "You hate all who do iniquity. You destroy those who speak falsehood; the LORD abhors the man of bloodshed and deceit" (Psalms 5:5-6). Sometimes just a general category is mentioned: "Everyone who Acts unjustly is an abomination to the LORD your God" (Deuteronomy 25:16). Sometimes a specific kind of sinner is singled out: "The LORD tests the righteous and the wicked, and the one who loves violence His soul hates" (Psalms 11:5). The seven things that God hates in Proverbs 6:16-19 include "a false witness who utters lies, and one who spreads strife among brothers." He also hates "the perverse in heart" (Proverbs 11:20), "everyone who is proud in heart" (Proverbs 16:5), and whoever justifies the wicked or condemns the righteous (Proverbs 17:15).

Other passages describe God's hatred for specific persons. Leviticus 20:23 speaks of God as abhorring or loathing the Canaanites. Sometimes his hatred is directed against Israel: "He was filled with wrath, and greatly abhorred Israel" when he saw her idolatry (Psalms 78:59). "I have come to hate her," he says (Jeremiah 12:8; cf. Hosea 9:15). He also hated Esau (Edom), says Malachi 1:3 (cf. Romans 9:13).

We cannot take these passages lightly. To be hated by the holy God is a terrible, terrifying thing. The Old Testament word translated "to hate" expresses "an emotional attitude toward persons and things which are opposed, detested, and despised, and with which one wishes to have no contact or relationship. It is therefore the opposite of love. Whereas love draws and unites, hate separates and keeps distant. The hated and hating persons are considered foes or enemies and are considered odious, utterly unappealing" (G. Van Gronigen, *Theological Wordbook of the Old Testament* [Moody 1980], II:880). Could anything be more terrifying than to hear God say, "I hate you"?

Nevertheless, we must remember that God hates the sinner *yet loves the sinner* at the same time! This is what I call a "terrible tension" within the nature of God, a tension that could be resolved ONLY by the incarnation of God the Son and His propitiatory sacrifice of Himself on the cross. In Christ's death as our substitute, both God's wrath against sinners and His love for sinners are perfectly expressed and fulfilled.

(This material is mostly from my book, *What the Bible Says About God the Redeemer* [College Press, 1987; now published by Wipf and Stock], pp. 286-287.)

DOES GOD HAVE A SENSE OF HUMOR?

QUESTION: Does God have a sense of humor?

ANSWER: This question could be taken in different ways. If one means, is he a comedian or joke-teller or practical joker, the answer is probably NO. Or someone might mean, does he have a sense of irony, as some answers to prayer seem to suggest. If this is the point, the answer is a definite PROBABLY. Finally, if one means, does he ever do or experience something akin to human laughter, the answer is certainly YES.

Some think they detect humor in some of Jesus' interactions with others as recorded in the Gospels. For example, Elton Trueblood wrote a book called *The Humor of Christ* (Harper & Row, 1964). One might consider a statement such as Matthew 23:24, "You blind guides, straining out a gnat and swallowing a camel!" The condemnation of hypocrisy is very serious, but the imagery called to mind by the illustration would surely evoke a smile. (I just googled "humor of Christ." The first page of references says there are 150,000,000 results.) [I tried again in July 2018. The number of results reported this time is 9,700,000.]

In the Bible, specific references to God laughing are Psalms 2:4; 37:15; 59:8; but these refer to the laughter of scorn or scoffing, not true humor. The rebellion and wickedness of sinners is not humorous, but it IS ridiculous--as if they think they can get away with it, or "put one over on God" thereby.

On the other hand, Luke 15:10 says when a sinner repents there is JOY in the presence of the angels. It does not specifically say the angels as such are rejoicing (though they no doubt are), but someone *in their PRESENCE*. Who is in their presence? GOD. I conclude that it is God who rejoices when a sinner repents, and his rejoicing must include at least a smile! I'm not sure this qualifies as a "sense of humor," but it surely signifies joy and happiness.

THE SHACK: THE GOOD, THE BAD, AND THE UGLY
An Analysis by Jack Cottrell

I wrote this analysis of *The Shack*, a novel by William P. Young, in March 2009; but as far as I can remember, it has not been published anywhere exactly like this. It was first written in an outline form, and I have tried to convert it here into essay form. The page numbers refer to an early edition: Windblown Media (Los Angeles, 2007). I did not see the 2017 movie version; I do not know how faithfully it corresponds to the original book.

I. THE STORY LINE

As a boy Mackenzie Phillips—"Mack"—was severely abused and beaten by his father. He ran away from home at age 13, grew up, became a decent man, attended a seminary, moved to Oregon, married, held a good job, and maintained a nominal interest in God and religion. When the story begins Mack is about 50 years old, has five children with three still home, including a young daughter Melissa (Missy), who is about 6 ½ years old. Missy becomes the victim of a serial child killer, who takes her to a tumble-down shack on a lake in a deep forest, where Missy's blood-soaked dress is later found. Mack descends into "Great Sadness."

About three years later Mack gets a strange note in his mailbox: "Mackenzie: It's been a while. I've missed you. I'll be at the shack next weekend if you want to get together. – Papa." "Papa" is the wife's nickname for God. Is it a cruel hoax, or is it really from God? How could it be from God?

Mack feels compelled to go to the shack, unsure of what he would find. He enters it and finds only the original bloodstain. In a rage he trashes the shack, and says to God, "I hate you!" "Some 'Papa' you are!" On his way back to his vehicle, everything changes, and Mack finds himself in an alternate universe. Winter turns into a beautiful summer scene all around him. The shack becomes a lovely, sturdy log cabin. All is "postcard perfect" (81): smoke coming from the chimney, the sound of laughter. Mack returns to the cabin and is about to knock when he meets God face to face.

II. WHAT MACK FOUND IN "THE SHACK"

When Mack entered the shack he found the three persons of the Trinity in distinct theophanies.

God the Father—"Papa"—is in the form of a large, beaming African-American woman. God the Son is the fully-human Jesus wearing tools and covered with wood dust: a carpenter. God the Holy Spirit is a small, wiry Asian woman named Sarayu (Sanskrit for air, wind). Mack asks, "Which one of you is God?" "'I am,' said all three in unison" (87).

God's purpose, by means of this direct encounter, was to straighten Mack out, to lift away his "great sadness" by explaining to him the true nature of God and the true meaning of all things. The solution to all the world's problems is summed up in one word: LOVE (or *loving relationships*).

Mankind was originally created *for* love and *to* love. The Trinity is the original love relationship (101-102). "We created you, the human, to … join our circle of love" (124).

But the original human beings had free will, and they used it not to *love* but to assert their own *independence*. This was the FALL. It ruined everything. Now God is working to *restore/redeem* creation via the power of love. He is leading all to reounce everything that negates love and to enter into loving relationships with everyone. Mack himself needs to "get right" with God, with his own father, and with Missy's killer.

III. WHAT JACK [YOUR REVIEWER] FINDS IN *THE SHACK*

Now that we have summarized the book's story line, we can proceed to analyze and critique its contents in the light of the Bible. My general conclusion is that it contains a mixture of good and bad, as in the nursery rhyme:

> *There was a little girl who had a little curl,*
> *right in the middle of her forehead.*
> *When she was good, she was very, very good;*
> *but when she was bad, she was horrid.*

Or, walking in the footsteps of Clint Eastwood, we find the good, the bad, and the ugly.

A.   The GOOD

The book affirms many of the usual attributes of God, e.g., transcendence (101), infinity (98), immutability (97-98), eternity (172), omnipresence (195), omniscience (91), foreknowledge (90, 99). God's foreknowledge is not in conflict with free will. Papa says: "I don't wonder what you will do or what choices you will make. I already know" (186-187; cf. 94, 222). Especially emphasized are goodness, love, and grace (see below). Papa says: "If you knew I was good and that everything … is all covered by my goodness, then … you would trust me" (126).

The book affirms a doctrine of the Trinity that sees three distinct persons who are equally divine. Papa: "I am one God and I am three persons, and each of the three is fully and entirely the one" (101). There are no hints of Unitarianism (as in modalism), or of Arianism. Jesus Himself is both fully God and fully man. Papa: "Jesus is fully human" and "he is also fully God" (99). Jesus: "I am fully God, but I am human to the core" (112).

The basic approach to the problem of evil—a major theme of the book—is pretty close to the best view, i.e., the "free will defense." Out of love God created human beings with free will; all evil comes from free human choices. God does not intervene at every potential sin. That would violate love (145). But God will bring good out of it all at the end. Papa: "I will use every choice you make for the ultimate good and the most loving outcome" (125). "Everything … is all covered by my goodness" (126). "I work incredible good out of unspeakable tragedies" (185). On the surface this sounds a lot like Romans 8:28. (This will be discussed further below.)

B. The BAD

Almost everything bad in *The Shack* stems from the key thesis that LOVE is the only true reality, or the only thing that matters. All the world's problems are seen as stemming from a failure to relate to all others in love; all problems can be solved by a return to LOVE.

Thus the fundamental error throughout the book is the misrepresentation of the nature of God as LOVE ONLY. This is serious false doctrine, and I have taught against it my entire career. The very essence of Christianity depends upon distinguishing TWO sides within God's moral nature, and in seeing them as equally ultimate. The two sides are (1) *love* (mercy, grace) and (2) *holiness* (wrath, retribution). See Romans 11:22, "Behold then the kindness and severity of God." See my book, *What the Bible Says About God the Redeemer* (College Press 1987), chapters 5 and 6. Seeing God as *love only* is a serious error in itself; it also leads to many other false doctrines, as will be seen below.

In the book, this "love is everything" thesis is why the *Trinity* is important: this is why God IS love, and why love and relationship are inherent in God. Papa: "All love and relationship is possible for you *only* because it already exists within Me, within God myself … . I *am* love" (101).

This is true enough, but—I will say it again—here is the key problem: *The Shack* sees God as love ONLY. Papa: "The God who is—the I who am I—cannot act apart from love" (102). But Romans 11:22 says we should "consider therefore the kindness **and severity** [or **sternness**] of God." The book, however does not see it this way. See this exchange between Mack and Papa (186): Mack: "But I always liked Jesus better than you. He seemed so gracious and you seemed so …" Papa: "Mean? Sad, isn't it? He came to show people who I am and most folks only believe it about him. They still play us off like good cop/bad cop most of the time, especially the religious folk. When they want people to do what they think is right, they need a stern God. When they need forgiveness, they run to Jesus … . But we were all in him. He reflected my heart exactly."

God's holiness is just folded into or blended into God's love, not distinguished from it. As Mack observes the pure love between Jesus and Papa, he realizes that this is what true holiness really is: "something simple, warm, intimate, genuine … . Holiness had always been a cold and sterile concept to Mack, but *this* was neither" (107-108).

According to *The Shack*, God's anger is just one way his love expresses itself (118-119): "You seem to be especially fond of a lot of people," Mack observed with a suspicious look. "Are there any who you are *not* especially fond of?" She [Papa] lifted her head and rolled her eyes as if she were mentally going through the catalogue of every being ever created. "Nope, I haven't been able to find any. Guess that's jes' the way I is." Mack was interested. "Do you ever get mad at any of them?" "Sho 'nuff! What parent doesn't? There is a lot to be mad about in the mess my kids have made and in the mess they're in. I don't like a lot of choices they make, but that anger—especially for me—is an expression of love all the same. I love the ones I am angry with just as much as those I'm not."

Mack challenges this: "But what about your wrath? It seems to me that if you're going to pretend to be God Almighty, you need to be a lot angrier … . Weren't you always running around killing people in the Bible? You just don't seem to fit the bill" (119). He continues, "But if you are God, aren't you the one spilling out great bowls of wrath and throwing people into a burning lake of fire? … Honestly, don't you enjoy punishing those who disappoint you?"

At that, Papa turned toward Mack. He could see a deep sadness in her eyes. "I am not who you think I am, Mackenzie. I don't need to punish people for sin. Sin is its own punishment, devouring you from the inside. It's not my purpose to punish it; it's my joy to cure it" (119-120).

One seriously false implication *The Shack* draws from the thesis that love is the only true reality is this: *Law* and *rules* are inconsistent with love. Loving relationships and rule following simply do not mix. See the conversation between Mack and Sarayu on pp. 197-198.

Mack: "It feels like living out of relationship—you know, trusting and talking to you—is a bit more complicated than just following rules." …

Sarayu: "Mackenzie!" she chided, her words flowing with affection. "The Bible doesn't teach you to follow rules. It is a picture of Jesus." …

Mack: "But you gotta admit, rules and principles are simpler than relationships."

Sarayu: "It is true that relationships are a whole lot messier than rules, but rules will never give you the answers to the deep questions of the heart and they will never love you."

Mack: "So, will I see you again?" he asked hesitantly.

Sarayu: "Of course. You might see me in a piece of art, or music, or silence, or through people, or in Creation, or in your joy and sorrow. My ability to communicate is limitless, living and transforming, and it will always be tuned to Papa's goodness and love. And you will hear and see me in the Bible in fresh ways. Just don't look for rules and principles; look for relationship— a way of coming to be with us."

Note: this entire conversation commits the logical fallacy of FALSE CHOICE. Rules and relationships are not a matter of *either/or*, but *both/and*. Jesus said, "If you love me, you will obey what I command" (John 14:15). But *The Shack* says, when we learn to share the *life of love* with God and others, we don't need law. In fact, says Sarayu, "In Jesus you are not under any law. All things are lawful" (203). Actually, says Sarayu, Jesus fulfilled all the law for you "so that it no longer has jurisdiction over you … . Jesus laid the demand of the law to rest." Mack replies, "Are you saying I don't have to follow the rules?" Sarayu: "Yes. In Jesus you are not under any law. All things are lawful … ." (202-203).

The result of all this is just another version of Joseph Fletcher's original "situation ethics": love gives us the freedom to respond in any situation (1) without rules and requirements, without being *supposed* to do a certain thing; (2) without expectation that we should respond in a specific way; and (3) without responsibility. See 205-206:

> Papa: "Honey, I've never placed an expectation on you or anyone else … . And beyond that, because I have no expectations, you never disappoint me."
>
> "What? You've never been disappointed in me?" Mack was trying hard to digest this.
>
> "Never!" Papa stated emphatically. "What I do have is a constant and living expectancy in our relationship, and I give you an ability to respond to any situation and circumstance in which you find yourself. To the degree that you resort to expectations and responsibilities, to that degree you neither know me nor trust me."

My analysis is that this shows a serious failure to understand the difference between law and grace as ways of salvation, and is a serious distortion of Paul's teaching that we are not under law but under grace (Romans 6:14). When Paul says "you are not under law but under grace," he is contrasting the law *system* of salvation with the grace *system* of salvation. In relationship with Jesus we are not under the law *system*, but under the grace system. But there is a serious difference between the law *system* and a law *code*. Even though we as Christians are not under the law as a system of salvation, we are still under a law CODE as a way of life. Even though we are *justified* by faith and not by works done in obedience to our law code (Romans 3:28), we are still absolutely obligated to obey our law code. Such obedience to law commandments is the essence of *sanctification*.

The false thesis that loving relationships are the only true reality leads to another seriously false conclusion, namely, to the condemnation of all authority, hierarchy, and true submission as being illegitimate. In other words, *The Shack* draws the conclusion that love requires the universal application of the irrational concept of "mutual submission."

This question comes up in relation to how the persons of the Trinity relate. Mack says, "Isn't one of you more the boss than the other two? ... I have always thought of God the Father as sort of being the boss and Jesus as the one following orders," with the Spirit being also "under the direction of the Father." "Don't you have a chain of command?" (121-122). The Trinity's answer: That's ridiculous! "We have no concept of final authority among us, only unity. We are in a *circle* of relationship, not a chain of command ... . Hierarchy would make no sense among us" (122). Why is it so wrong?

Because authority and hierarchy destroy relationships. Jesus says, "Hierarchy imposes laws and rules and you end up missing the wonder of relationship that we intended for you" (122-3). All such hierarchy is the result of the Fall. "Humans are so lost and damaged that to you it is almost incomprehensible that people could work or live together without someone being in charge" (122).

Sarayu explains: "Authority, as you usually think of it, is merely the excuse the strong use to make others conform to what they want" (123).

The bottom line is that the relationship among the persons of the Trinity, which is presented as the model for all personal relationships, is a kind of "mutual submission." Jesus says, "That's the beauty you see in my relationship with Abba and Sarayu. We are indeed submitted to one another and have always been so and always will be. Papa is as much submitted to me as I to him, or Sarayu to me, or Papa to her. Submission is not about authority and it is not obedience; it is all about relationships of love and respect" (145).

(Here I will pause to say that this concept of submission is completely twisted and redefined, and retains none of the meaning of the New Testament Greek word for submission.)

But, says *The Shack*, this novel interpretation of "mutual" submission applies not only to the persons of the Trinity, but also to the God-man relationship. Jesus says to Mack, concerning the Trinity, "We are submitted to you in the same way." Mack: "How can that be? Why would the God of the universe want to be submitted to me?" (145). Jesus: "Because we want you to join us in our circle of relationship. I don't want slaves to my will; I want brothers and sisters who will share life with me" (146).

The Shack also applies this concept of mutual submission to all human relationships, especially to husbands and wives. Mack is dubious of the idea: "Every human institution that I can think of, from political to business, even down to marriage, is governed by this kind of thinking [i.e., submission and authority]; it is the web of our social fabric." Papa's reply: "Such a waste!" (122). When Jesus explains mutual submission to Mack, he replies: "And that's how you want us to love each other ... ? I mean between husbands and wives, parents and children, I guess in any relationship?" Jesus: "Exactly! When I am your life, submission is the most natural expression of my character and nature, and it will be the most natural expression of your new nature within relationships"(146).

Male headship is specifically described as the result of the Fall in Eden, when Adam and Eve traded relationship for independence. Mack: "I've always wondered why men have been in charge ... . Males seem to be the cause of so much of the pain in the world" (146-7). Jesus says to forget about gender *roles*. "Mack, don't you see how filling roles is the opposite of relationship? We want male and female to be counterparts, face-to-face equals," and "fully equal" (148).

By way of analysis, I must now ask how this relates to Biblical teaching. One of the biggest issues among Evangelicals today is whether there is an eternal relationship of subordination within the Trinity and how this affects gender roles. But *eternal* subordination is not the issue, since Scripture is clear that in the *incarnation* Jesus as the Son did take upon Himself such a submissive role in relation to the Father, which is the model for male headship and female submission (1 Corinthians 11:3). Jesus's incarnational role of submission to the Father's will (John 4:34; 6:38; Hebrews 10:7) gives us the true understanding of authority and submission, contrary to "mutual submission."

The whole concept of "mutual submission" is a verbal and conceptual oxymoron, a human invention without any basis in Scripture whatsoever, created *ex nihilo* by feminists to explain away texts such as Ephesians 5:22-24. I have discussed these issues thoroughly in my book, *Headship, Submission, and the Bible: Gender Roles in the Home* (College Press, 2008; 334pp., pb.).

An apparent implication of *The Shack*'s unrelenting emphasis on loving relationships is universal salvation. This comes out in the book's ultimate purpose, i.e., to offer hope in the presence of *evil*, to try to help people deal with the problem of evil and suffering. The basic explanation is this: God created everything for the purpose of love (loving relationships), which requires free will; but human beings distorted everything by using their free will to sin. Nevertheless, God will still see that his purpose of love is fulfilled, in spite of pain, murder, etc.

E.g., Papa says to Mack: "We want to share with you the love and joy and freedom and light that we already know within ourself. We created you, the human, to be in face-to-face relationship with us, to join our circle of love. As difficult as it will be for you to understand, everything that has taken place is occurring exactly according to this purpose, without violating choice or will" (124-5). God will use every human choice—even those involving pain, war, and child murder—to accomplish his purpose. The following exchange ensues:

Papa: "Your choices are not stronger than my purposes, and I will use every choice you make for the ultimate good and the most loving outcome ... . Everything—the means, the ends, and all the processes of individual lives—is all covered by my goodness" (125-6).

Mack: "One last comment. I just can't imagine any final outcome that would justify all this."

Papa: "Mackenzie. We're not justifying it. We are redeeming it" (127).

At first this *sounds* a lot like Romans 8:28: "We know that God causes all things to work together for good to those who love God, to those who are called according to His purpose." As Papa says, "Just because I work incredible good out of unspeakable tragedies doesn't mean I orchestrate the tragedies" (185). A major difference, though, is that in Romans 8:28 this promise is NOT made to everyone, but only to the saints (v. 27), those who love God and who have answered his call. *The Shack*, however, *universalizes* this promise, thus opening the door to universal salvation.

Such universalism is implied by the basic idea that God's ultimate nature is goodness and love. In a kind of judgment scene, a female figure (Sophia) shows Mack that he is judging God for not judging child killers. She challenges Mack: "You must choose two of your children to spend eternity in God's new heavens and new earth," and three "to spend eternity in hell." Mack couldn't believe what he was hearing and started to panic. "Mackenzie. I am only asking you to do something that you believe God does ... . You believe he will condemn most to an eternity of torment, away from His presence and apart from His love. Is that not true?" Mack replies, "I suppose I do ... . I just assumed that somehow God could do that." Sophia: "So you suppose, then, that God does this easily, but you cannot? Come now, Mackenzie. Which three of your five children will you sentence to hell?" Well, Mack just could not do it. There was simply no way he could sentence any of his children to an eternity in hell just because they had sinned against him, or even committed some heinous crime. He couldn't! For him, it wasn't about their performance; it was about his love for them. Here is Sophia's reply: "And now you know Papa's heart, who loves all his children perfectly" (161-163). "I don't do … condemnation," says Papa (223).

This is where the cross comes in. Papa asks, why did Jesus go to the cross? "For love. He chose the way of the cross where mercy triumphs over justice because of love. Would you instead prefer he'd chosen justice for everyone?" (164-165). Papa says in another place, "Evil is the chaos of this age that you brought to me, but it will not have the final say" (190). Sophia contributes this: "This life is only the anteroom of a greater reality to come. No one reaches their potential in your world. It's only preparation for what Papa had in mind all along" (167).

Papa relates this to the cross again: "Like I said, everything is about him. Creation and history are all about Jesus. He is the very center of our purpose and in him we are now fully human, so our purpose and your destiny are forever linked. You might say that we have put all our eggs in the one human basket. There is no plan B." This led to the following conversation.

> "Seems pretty risky," Mack surmised.
>
> "Maybe for you, but not for me. There has never been a question that what I wanted from the beginning, I will get. Honey, you asked me what Jesus accomplished on the cross; so now listen to me carefully: through his death and resurrection, I am now fully reconciled to the world."
>
> "The whole world? You mean those who believe in you, right?"
>
> "The whole world, Mack. All I am telling you is that reconciliation is a two way street, and I have done my part, totally, completely, finally. It is not the nature of love to force a relationship but it is the nature of love to open up the way" (192). "In Jesus, I have forgiven all humans for their sins against me, but only some choose relationship" (225). "It's not my purpose to punish sin" (120).

This is why we forgive even child killers. Papa tells Mack that he (Mack) will one day completely forgive Missy's killer. "And then one day you will pray for his wholeness and give him over to me so that my love will burn from his life every vestige of corruption" (227).

Contrary to all such vain hopes of universal salvation, see my book, *The Faith Once for All* (College Press, 2002), chapter 33, on the reality and eternality of hell.

C. THE UGLY

The Shack presents a basically orthodox view of the *person* of Christ: he is fully God and fully man (99, 112). But here is a serious qualification with regard to Christ's *work*: although Jesus is fully God, "he has *never* drawn upon his nature as God to do anything" (99). The implications are devastating. In essence, Jesus is stripped of His power to redeem us.

This book completely negates the power of Christ to be an atonement for sin. See the following exchange. Mack says, "What exactly did Jesus accomplish by dying?" Papa: "Oh, nothing much. Just the substance of everything that love purposed from before the foundations of Creation" (191). I.e., "Through his death and resurrection, I am now fully reconciled to the world" (192).

The problem is that *The Shack* never explains HOW the cross accomplishes the purpose of love. It affirms that he did it "for love," and in so doing "mercy triumphs over justice because of love" (164).

But there is no explanation of why or how the cross was necessary for accomplishing this.

The Bible, however, makes this all clear: God is love (1 John 4:8), but He is not *love only*. He is also a "consuming fire," the fire of wrath (Hebrews 12:29). The righteous God must pour out His wrath upon sinners to satisfy the demands of His holy nature; but His own love has provided Jesus as a substitute for sinners, to receive God's wrath in our place. This is the sense in which the cross is a propitiation (Romans 3:24-26; 1 John 4:10), an offering by means of which Jesus turns God's wrath away from us by taking it upon Himself. The cross thus allows God to forgive believing sinners and still be righteous. (See Cottrell, *The Faith Once for All*, ch. 14; and Cottrell, *God the Redeemer*, ch. 7.)

But *The Shack*'s God is *love only*; he has no real wrath, and he does not punish sin. When God is viewed thus, the whole rationale and purpose for the cross must be drastically changed. In fact, it becomes difficult to provide any rationale at all for it. This is why Papa can say with such finality that even though Jesus is God, "he has *never* drawn upon his nature as God to do anything" (99). This must mean that even on the cross, Jesus was dying only as a human being, and that His divine nature was not involved.

The atonement is thus stripped of its power. In his finite human nature alone, Jesus could never have atoned for all the sins of all people. But as our substitute He *did* suffer the equivalent of eternity in hell for every individual—an infinite quantity of suffering. He could do this only if His divine nature, which itself is infinite, participated in the atonement. This is why God (the Son) became a human being in the first place. To say that He never drew upon His divine nature to do anything negates the whole purpose of the incarnation and the whole power of the atonement. See Cottrell, *God the Redeemer*, 509-516.

The principle that Jesus never draws upon His divine nature for anything actually negates His uniqueness altogether. That He exists and operates only through His full unity and relationship with the Father just makes Him the prototype or model for all humanity. Everything He did and does as a human being is simply what God expects of all human beings. Says Papa of Jesus: "He has only lived out of his relationship with me, living in the very same manner that I desire to be in relationship with every human being. He is just the first to do it to the uttermost—the first to absolutely trust my life within him, the first to believe in my love and my goodness without regard for appearance or consequence." "Only as he rested in his relationship with me, and in our communion—our co-union—could he express my heart and will into any given circumstance ... . That's how he lives and Acts as a true human, how every human is designed to live—out of my life" (99-100).

My conclusion is this: As a novel *The Shack* is a creative project and interesting reading.

However, the religious teaching it contains is such a mixture of good and bad that anyone reading it for spiritual benefit is in danger of being deceived in many serious ways.

PART TWO

THE WORKS OF GOD

GOD'S ETERNAL PURPOSE

INTRODUCTION

When you pick up your Bible and begin reading it from the beginning, you are immediately confronted with one of the most profound truths and most fundamental facts: "In the beginning God created the heavens and the earth." When you read this statement, it should immediately cause you to ask a very familiar and most important question: "WHY?" **Why** did God create the heavens and the earth? It was not just an accident, or a whim. He *chose* to do it. In Revelation 4:11, angelic beings worship God by saying, "You created all things, and **by your will** they existed and were created." Thus He must have had some kind of reason or *purpose*.

I have been thinking about this recently because I have been teaching Paul's letter to the Ephesians in our Sunday night church service here in Greendale, IN. In studying this letter, I have noticed how strongly Paul is emphasizing this theme of GOD'S ETERNAL PURPOSE.

In thinking about this, we must begin even before the "beginning" of Genesis 1:1. This earlier setting for God's formulating his eternal purpose is his pre-creation existence as the Trinity whom we know as the Father, the Son, and the Holy Spirit. Whatever else was happening then, God made a *decision*; He laid out a *plan* to do something, to accomplish something. In Ephesians 1:4ff. Paul refers to what God was doing "before the foundation of the world." (This is why this purpose is called an "eternal" purpose: it happened "in eternity," before this universe began.) In 1:5-11 Paul uses *six* different Greek words meaning "to purpose, to plan, to counsel, to will." See the following (from the ESV):

- "He predestined us for adoption through Jesus Christ according to the PURPOSE [*eudokia*] of his WILL" [*thelēma*] (1:5).

- He lavished grace upon us, "making known to us the mystery of his WILL [*thelēma* again], according to his PURPOSE [*protithēmi*], which he set forth in Christ" (1:9).

- "As a PLAN [*oikonomia*] for the fullness of time, to unite all things in" Christ (1:10).

- This was "according to the PURPOSE [*prothesis*] of him who works all things according to the COUNSEL [*boulē*] of his WILL [*thelēma* one more time]" (1:11).

Paul uses this language again in Ephesians 3:9, when he speaks of "the PLAN [*oikonomia*] of the mystery hidden for ages in God who created all things"; and in 3:11, "This was according to the ETERNAL PURPOSE [*prothesis*] that he has realized in Christ Jesus our Lord."

These texts alone show that God certainly has an ETERNAL PURPOSE. In this study *my* plan is to point out and explain three things: (1) What IS God's eternal purpose? (2) By what MEANS does He propose to bring it about? (3) What is the FULFILLMENT of this purpose?

I.   WHAT IS GOD'S ETERNAL PURPOSE?

One reason this is an important subject is that Ephesians 1 is a key Calvinist proof text for their most fundamental doctrine, namely, that the sovereignty of God means that he is the absolute CAUSE of every aspect of reality. Calvinists think this is taught in Ephesians 1:11, in the statement that God "works all things according to the counsel of his will." They assume that in this statement, the phrase "God works" means "God CAUSES." (The word translated "works" is *energeō*.) They say that "all things" is universal and comprehensive; it embraces everything with regard to the smallest and greatest events, with no exceptions — as if the context of this statement in Ephesians does not matter.

This is the beginning point of the Calvinist world view. The fundamental assumption and most basic doctrine of Calvinism is that divine sovereignty must be understood as absolute, all-inclusive *causation*. I sum it up as *omnicausal* (or *pancausal*) *sovereignty*.

Thus this text is used (by Calvinists) to prove that everything that happens is part of God's eternal purpose. The error in this, however, is that Calvinism does not understand that this statement is referring to one specific purpose, which is Paul's intended teaching. It fragments the "purpose" into a near-infinite number of purposes that are not necessarily related to one another. I.e., it is God's purpose to cause a specific leaf to fall from a specific tree at a specific time. It is God's purpose to cause a student to watch NCIS on TV rather than to do his homework. It is God's purpose to cause a specific butterfly to fly within striking distance of a specific chameleon's tongue in the middle of nowhere. It is God's purpose to cause you to pour exactly 472 Cheerios into your bowl for breakfast on a given morning. And so on, *ad infinitum.*

In terms of hermeneutics I describe this as the "shotgun" approach to Paul's statement. In case someone may think that I am exaggerating, here are some examples of this pancausalist view, cited from Calvinist sources.

A. John Piper

Not long ago I watched a brief internet video of John Piper answering this question: "Has God pre-determined every tiny detail in the universe, such as dust particles in the air and including all our sins?" Piper paused for a few seconds and then solemnly said: "Yes." He went on to explain about dust particles and sins, including the worst sin ever committed: Judas's betrayal of Christ. Whatever happens, happens because God CAUSES it to happen in order to fulfill his "eternal purpose."

Here are two comments on this. ONE, it makes sense to include Judas's betrayal of Jesus in God's eternal purpose, but to equate this with (e.g.) a specific dust particle landing on an obscure windowsill in Podunk KY on any given day requires fantastic mental gymnastics. TWO, it is interesting that Piper uses Judas' betrayal as an example of how God "works" all things according to the counsel of His will, as if God *caused* Judas to do everything he did. However, in Acts 2:23, the Apostle Peter says that Jesus was betrayed by "the definite plan [*boulē*] and **foreknowledge** of God." This suggests that God works things into His plan that He does not *cause*, but which He *foreknows* will happen by creatures' free-will choices.

B. William Hendriksen

In *New Testament Commentary: Ephesians* (Baker, 1967), William Hendriksen comments thus on Ephesians 1:11. "This plan ... includes absolutely all things that ever take place in heaven, on earth, and in hell; past, present, and even the future, pertaining to both believers and unbelievers, to angels and devils, to physical as well as spiritual energies and units of existence both large and small; he also *wholly carries it out*" (88). Also, "Everything is included in God's universe-embracing plan" (88-89). "God's decree from eternity is thus all-embracing" (89). Regarding Paul's reference to God's "eternal purpose" in Ephesians 3:11, Hendriksen says, "It governs the ages in all their continuity and contents" (160).

C. Louis Berkhof

In his *Systematic Theology* (Banner of Truth Trust, 1939/1941), Louis Berkhof uses Ephesians 1:11 to say that God's "sovereign will" is "the final cause of all things ... even the smallest things of life." "The will of God is the ultimate cause of all things" (76). This verse is cited as teaching that God "has sovereignly determined from all eternity whatsoever comes to pass, and works His sovereign will in His entire creation, both natural and spiritual, according to His predetermined plan" (100). This "predetermined plan" takes the form of God's "eternal decree," which predetermines every single thing that will ever happen. The decree is eternal, efficacious, immutable, and unconditional (102-105). Berkhof uses Ephesians 1:11 to assert that the decree is universal and all-comprehensive, that it includes whatever comes to pass, including all sins (105).

D. Wayne Grudem

In his *Systematic Theology* (Zondervan, 1994), Wayne Grudem says the same thing. He cites Ephesians 1:11 as proof that God's will is "the final or most ultimate reason for everything that happens" (211). Also, we cannot ignore "the clearly cosmic scope of the context" in the previous verse (342, n. 52).

E. John Eadie

Here is a final quote, from John Eadie's *Commentary on the Epistle to the Ephesians* (Zondervan reprint of 1883 edition, p. 60), where he says this of Ephesians 1:11: "This divine fore-resolve is universal in its sweep" — it means *all things*. It is "the plan of the universe." God's "undeviating purpose" is "seen alike whether He create a seraph or form a gnat—fashion a world or round a grain of sand—prescribe the orbit of a planet or the gyration of an atom. The extinction of a world and the fall of a sparrow are equally the result of a free pre-arrangement."

How may we respond to this Calvinist view, especially in view of Paul's statement in Ephesians 1:11, that "God works all things according to the counsel of his will"? Here I will say two things. First, even if we take "all things" to be all-inclusive, this text does not say God CAUSES everything, but that He WORKS everything in relation to His will. God "causes" some things, and has absolute *foreknowledge* of how everything else will proceed, even human free-will choices. He works all of this together into the pattern of His choice. For example, see Acts 2:23 again.

Second and mainly: Calvinism is wrong to take the "shotgun" approach to Paul's language and teaching here in Ephesians, which they do when they apply "all things" to the entire scope of reality. As we have seen, Calvinists try to include every atom and iota as the content of the purpose (plan, will, counsel) of God. They say it is cosmic, universal, comprehensive, all-inclusive.

But the Ephesians context of Paul's statement shows that this is *seriously wrong theology!* The purpose and plan of God that Paul is writing about here is very specific, like a rifle that is pointing at a single target. The eternal purpose is very focused. Paul is not suggesting that God has a unique purpose for every dust particle or snowflake, nor is he suggesting that every dust particle or snowflake somehow works into the one specific purpose on which He is focusing. Paul is concerned with the ONE purpose (singular) that God is pursuing, and the context of Ephesians will show us exactly what purpose Paul has in mind here. The point of Paul's statement is that God governs and controls *all things that are necessary to bring about this specific plan.* God will do *whatever it takes* to fulfill His specific purpose.

As a parallel, we can look at one other text in the New Testament that uses the very same language ("God works all things") in a limited way as determined by the context. In 1 Corinthians 12:6 Paul says that there are many kinds of spiritual gifts (ministries, works), but the same God "works all things in all people." The verb is the same as Ephesians 1:11 [*energeō*], and he uses the word "all" twice—but with limitations imposed by the context. See especially vv. 7-10, and see how Paul uses "all *these* things" (*panta tauta*) in verse 11, clearly referring to spiritual gifts.

This leads us to ask: What IS this *specific* plan or eternal purpose that God is working out in human history, as Paul is thinking of it here in Ephesians? In a nutshell (or as looked at through a rifle scope), God's eternal purpose is to prepare for Himself a FAMILY of personal, free-will beings who will relate to Him in a fellowship of love as His own sons and daughters. His plan is to love them and bestow upon them untold riches and blessings, and to receive in return their love and devotion. (This is what we can call DIVINE FAMILY PLANNING.) Here is how this theme is presented here in the Ephesian letter:

- God is our **Father** (1:2; 2:18; 4:6), and we are His **children**: "Be imitators of God, as beloved children … Walk as children of light" (5:1, 8). This is opposed to being children of wrath and children of disobedience (2:3; 5:6).

- "He predestined us for **adoption** through Jesus Christ, according to the purpose of his will" (1:5). Other references to our being adopted (not in Ephesians) are Romans 8:15, 23; Galatians 4:5.

- We "are members of the **household** of God" (2:19).

- Our Father has promised us a great **inheritance**: 1:11, 14, 18; 3:6; 5:5. Compare this with Romans 8 (especially verses 14-19, 21, 23, 29).

Recognizing this focus of God's eternal purpose is crucial for understanding everything else in the Bible. This is the framework within which all biblical history and teaching are set. Of special importance is the fact that this concept LIMITS the "all things" in Ephesians 1:11, and thus undermines the Calvinist interpretation of this text. It shows the fallacy of the shotgun approach to hermeneutics. And it shows the specific target at which the rifle-sight of God's working is aimed.

II. BY WHAT MEANS DOES GOD EXPECT TO ACHIEVE THIS ETERNAL PURPOSE?

How did God propose to achieve this wonderful purpose? His initial desire, purpose, and plan was to bring His family into existence by means of CREATION, i.e., by creating from nothing an entire visible universe as the home for this family, beginning with its first parents, Adam and Eve. This is set forth in the first two chapters of Genesis. Of special importance here is the fact that in this universe, the human family alone was created **in the image of God** (Genesis 1:26-27). By this means God specifically designed us for personal interaction and family fellowship with himself.

The "wild card" in this plan was the fact that the kind of family God wanted required that the image of God built into every human being, including Adam and Eve, included FREE WILL. Why was free will required? Because free will is necessary for a relationship involving real *love*, and thus for a true and meaningful communion with God as a *family*. Thus free will is a key part of the image of God. As we know, God's inclusion of free will in His creation plan was a big risk, but it was worth it for love's sake.

As we also know, the sad truth is that Adam and Eve used this marvelous gift to *commit sin* (Genesis 3), and thereby lost family fellowship with God for themselves and all their descendants. This is when the human race became no longer children of God but children of wrath (Ephesians 2:3) and sons of disobedience (5:6). Thus God's initial and preferred means of achieving His eternal purpose—by creation—was aborted.

Does this mean that God's eternal purpose itself has failed? NO! In His omniscience God knew all the possible results of creating free-will beings, and in His foreknowledge He knew that this specific result would happen. Therefore God had already included in His eternal purpose an alternative means, a *back-up* method for achieving His purpose, namely, REDEMPTION! Most of the Bible (especially Genesis 12ff.) focuses on this.

The point is that the *means* by which God has *actually* accomplished his eternal purpose and thus has established his family is *the redeeming work of Jesus of Nazareth* (i.e., God the Son himself, incarnate as a human being). The Biblical narrative presents this in two stages. First, most of the Bible — from Genesis 12 to Malachi — is the account of how God *prepared* for the coming of the Redeemer. This is the history of the ethnic group chosen for this privilege, namely, Abraham's descendants through Isaac and Jacob, the Jews, the nation of Israel.

As a physical nation the Jews' purpose was to set the stage for the redemptive super-hero, Jesus the Messiah. Their purpose was to prepare the ground for the planting of the Seed. This was done by generating *holiness* through the *law*, and by generating *hope* through the *prophets*. The history of Israel boils down to this. However, as large and as important as this part of the Bible is, it is crucial that we understand that this was just *preparation* for the main event. Israel as a nation was NOT the family that is the goal of God's eternal purpose. When the Redeemer himself came, Israel's role in God's purpose was actually completed. (Paul shows this in Romans 9-11, as I explain in my commentary on this grand New Testament book.)

The *heart* of the Bible is the GOSPELS, which are the records of the fundamental yet alternative MEANS by which God is working out His eternal purpose, i.e., that means being the redemptive works of Jesus Christ. These redemptive works — His death, resurrection, ascension, and enthronement at the right hand of God — are why He came. His main task was not to reveal something to us, or to set a moral example for us, but to die and rise again for us! These are the works that enable God to fulfill his eternal purpose! Through them, children of disobedience and wrath can be forgiven and rehabilitated (repatriated, redeemed, reformed, restored, transformed) into CHILDREN OF GOD—THE FAMILY OF GOD—acceptable for eternal fellowship with God!

This is why Paul, especially in Ephesians, repeats over and over that God's purpose is accomplished only "in Christ Jesus," "through Jesus Christ," "in the Beloved," "through his blood," "in Christ," "in him, in him, in him, in him" — on and on. (See especially Ephesians 1:1-13.) As 3:11 says, "the eternal purpose" has been realized "in Christ Jesus our Lord."

III. THE ACTUAL FULFILLMENT OF GOD'S ETERNAL PURPOSE IS IN THE CHURCH.

Going back to the Old Testament for a moment, I affirm that God was saving believers in Old Testament times, but not with the *fullness* of salvation. What shall we say, then, about the saints of God especially from Abraham onward and those under the Law of Moses, even into the pre-Pentecost history recorded in the gospels? What about Abraham, and Moses, and David, and Isaiah, and Elizabeth and Zechariah, and John the Baptist? True — many Israelites (but not all) were true believers in the one true God and had forgiveness of their sins. And God said to Israel, over and over, "you are My people"! (See, e.g., Exodus 6:7; Leviticus 26:12; Jeremiah 30:22.) Were they not "God's family"?

Yes, they were — in one sense and to some degree. But Israel was NOT the family God had planned and envisioned from before the foundation of the world (1:4) as the family of His *eternal purpose*. In Old Testament times there was something about this "family" that was incomplete, something that was lacking, something that fell short of God's eternal purpose. This was a preliminary stage, a preparatory step toward the actual establishment of God's eternal family. For one thing, Israel was not a true *family*; they were more like a *nation*. More importantly, God dealt with Israel almost altogether on a *physical* level. And most significantly, even the saved among Israel did not have the *fullness* of salvation.

This last point is seen in Paul's reference in Ephesians to God's "purpose, which he set forth in Christ as a plan for the fullness of time" (1:10-11). He says in 1:3 that our God and Father "has blessed us **in Christ** with every **spiritual** blessing in the heavenly places." The bestowing of these spiritual blessings—and the establishment of God's family—began on the day of Pentecost. From Acts 2 to the end of the New Testament, we see God's eternal purpose being fulfilled!

The really big blessing, the new blessing, given for the first time on Pentecost, was the outpouring of the Holy Spirit, or as Ephesians 1:13 says, "the promised Holy Spirit." The new thing on Pentecost was NOT miracles such as speaking in tongues, and not even forgiveness of sins. The new thing was the gift of the indwelling of the Spirit, whose power works within us the spiritual blessings of regeneration and sanctification, and the sealing that marks us as members of God's eternal family (1:13)! He is the "Spirit of adoption as sons, by whom we cry, 'Abba! Father!'" (Romans 8:15). See Romans 8:14-17.

This new fullness of salvation means that God's people now have the full "double cure" of salvation. This includes not only the forgiveness of sins (Ephesians 1:7), which was already available and being experienced in the pre-Christian era. Now it includes the new thing — "that we should be holy and blameless before him" (Ephesians 1:4). This is what Paul explains in Ephesians 2:1-10 as resurrection from spiritual death to new spiritual life. This is the *new* creation—the "created in Christ Jesus" of Ephesians 2:10.

But there is yet one more thing that marks the transition from the Old Covenant era to the New Covenant era—one more thing that tells us that Old Testament Israel was not the family of God's pre-creation plan—one more thing that began in principle on the Day of Pentecost, to establish God's eternal family plan. This is what Paul refers to in Ephesians as the **MYSTERY** element of God's purpose—a mystery that he had kept hidden until the New Covenant era, a mystery that was just then being revealed through the New Testament apostles and prophets, namely, "the mystery of his will" (1:9). What is this mystery?

This goes back to the make-up of the human race in pre-Christian times. One result of God's separating the Jews as a nation from the rest of the world was this: the human race was divided into two categories—Jews and Gentiles. See Ephesians 2:11-12. (And remember in Old Testament times not even the Jews were a FAMILY before God. Another main reason for this is that most of the Jews were unbelievers! Only a remnant were true believers, and even they were not treated in a very special way compared to the non-believers.)

But this was temporary. God had a plan that would change this! He had a plan, but by design He did not reveal it clearly in Old Testament times. It was a mystery kept secret until the New Testament era, when God revealed it through His New Testament apostles and prophets, and especially through the Apostle Paul! The mystery has to do with the membership of the family of God.

What exactly is this mystery? Read Ephesians 3:1-9, as summed up in verse 6: "This mystery is that the Gentiles are fellow heirs, members of the same body, and partakers of the promise in Christ Jesus through the gospel" (ESV). The mystery now revealed is that in this New Covenant era, God has abolished the distinction between Jews and Gentiles! He has brought into existence something new — a "new man" — "ONE new man in place of two" (Ephesians 2:15).

In this way He has established a family — HIS family — that is composed not just of believing Israelites but also of believing Gentiles! We are all now "members of the household of God" (2:19). We are all now "fellow heirs" (3:6)!

How is this mystery *made known* to the world? It is "made known"— in the sense of announced and explained—via divine revelation, especially through Paul, but also through other New Testament prophets and apostles (Ephesians 3:3-5, 7-9). But if by "made known" we mean— becomes a reality that is visible to this whole world as well as to the angelic world, then the mystery of God's eternal purpose to have one united family of sons and daughters for eternity is brought to light THROUGH THE CHURCH! Read Ephesians 3:10-11.

The bottom line is that the New Testament church is God's eternal purpose accomplished! Through Jesus Christ, and in the very existence of his church, the eternal purpose of God has been brought to fulfillment. It is no accident that the origin of this new family of God is called an act of CREATION (*ktidzo*) in Ephesians 2:15, where Paul says that Jesus Christ has **created** in himself one new man in place of two. And every convert, through faith and in baptism, is "**created** in Christ Jesus for good works" (Ephesians 2:10). Thus God's family exists via creation after all — but via NEW creation. See 2 Corinthians 5:17 — "If anyone is in Christ, he is a new creation." We are "created in Christ Jesus for good works, which God prepared beforehand, that we should walk in them" (Ephesians 2:10). In this new creation we have "put on the new self, created after the likeness of God in true righteousness and holiness" (Ephesians 4:24). This was His plan all along! "He predestined us for adoption through Jesus Christ, according to the purpose of his will" (Ephesians 1:5).

As glorious as this church family is, we are now still in the transitional stage of it. We are indeed God's family on earth; see Romans 8:14-17; 2 Corinthians 6:16-18. But there is another stage—the final stage--yet to come! God's eternal purpose is not completed here on this earth! There is coming a day when ALL believers from ALL ages will be gathered together into one worldwide community—not only as redeemed souls but also in redeemed bodies—living as an eternal family in a new universe, the new heavens and new earth. That's when we will receive the true fullness of salvation, the full inheritance that God had planned for His family from the beginning. See Romans 8:18-25.

CONDITIONAL ELECTION

This essay is a systematic analysis of the Biblical teaching on election, sometimes referred to as predestation. The first thing we must do is define some terms. The word *predestine* or *predestinate* means "to determine or to decide beforehand, to determine the destiny of in advance, to foreordain to a particular end." This is a general term and can refer to things or to events, as well as to persons. The word *elect* means "to pick out, to choose," and it ordinarily refers to persons only. God's elect are the persons whom He chose before the foundation of the world. With reference to persons, the nouns *predestination* and *election* may be used interchangeably.

We may distinguish several types of election. First, there is election of individuals to an office or a task. Jesus said of His apostles, "Did I Myself not choose you, the twelve?" (John 6:70). The eternal destiny of the individual is not involved in this type of election; Jesus went on to say, "And *yet* one of you is a devil." Second, there is collective election, or the election of groups or nations to a certain end. God said to the nation Israel, "The LORD your God has chosen you to be a people for His own possession" (Deuteronomy 7:6). A careful study of the first three chapters of Ephesians shows that collective election is in the forefront in Paul's thinking here. The third type of election is individual election, which can refer to God's choosing someone strictly to serve a divine purpose (e.g., Pharaoh, Romans 9:17), or to God's predestination of individuals to eternal life. This last type is usually foremost in our minds when we think about the idea of predestination; therefore we shall be dealing here with this last type of election only, i.e., the predestination of individuals to eternal life.

We may ask first of all, is there such a thing as predestination? Does God determine beforehand the eternal destiny of human beings? Has God already decided who will be saved and who will be lost? Has God already determined whether you will be in heaven or not? The answer of all these questions is YES. It is necessary to ask such questions because so many people have equated predestination with a particular interpretation of it which is repulsive to them, and therefore they have rejected the whole idea as unscriptural. But it is taught in Scripture! And thus we must agree with John Calvin when he says, "Scripture is the school of the Holy Spirit, in which ... nothing is taught but what is expedient to know. Therefore we must guard against depriving believers of anything disclosed about predestination in Scripture, lest we seem ... wickedly to defraud them of the blessing of their God ..." (*Institutes of the Christian Religion*, III.xxi.3). "They who shut the gates that no one may dare seek a taste of this doctrine wrong men no less than God" (*ibid.*, III.xxi.1). We cannot agree, of course, with Calvin's *interpretation* of this Biblical teaching.

So our question here is this: How does God predetermine the eternal destiny of individuals? There are two basic answers to this question. The first is that election is unconditional. This means that God decides who will be saved for reasons completely within Himself and not on the basis of whether or not the individual has met certain conditions laid down by God. The Reformed document called the Westminster Confession of Faith (III:5) puts it this way:

> Those of mankind that are predestinated unto life, God, before the foundation of the world was laid, according to his eternal and immutable purpose, and the secret counsel and good pleasure of his will, hath chosen in Christ, unto everlasting glory, out of his mere free grace and love, without any foresight of faith or good works, or perseverance in either of them, or any other thing in the creature, as

conditions, or causes moving him thereunto, and all to the praise of his glorious grace.

The second answer is that election is conditional. This means that God decides who will be saved unto eternal life on the basis of His foreknowledge of whether individuals will meet the conditions which He Himself has laid down for salvation. Our thesis here is that Scripture teaches a conditional election, and our purpose is to explain it and to show its implications.

I. AN EXPLANATION OF CONDITIONAL ELECTION

We turn first of all to a fuller explanation of the idea of conditional election. The beginning point for the explanation is the statement in Ephesians 1:4, that God "chose us in Him," i.e., in Christ Jesus. Our Lord Jesus Christ is Himself *the* elect one, the individual chosen before time and world began, that He might be the Servant who would perform the work of salvation. In Isaiah 42:1 God says, "Behold, My Servant, whom I uphold; My chosen one *in whom* My soul delights." This is the beginning of the great servant passages in Isaiah, which reach their climax in the fifty-third chapter. Christ was chosen before the foundation of the world to perform the great work of atonement pictured therein. He was predestined to bear the sins of all mankind in His own body on the tree.

To say then that we are chosen "in Him" means that we are chosen on the basis of our relationship with Jesus Christ, *the* Chosen One. From the standpoint of eternity, God has foreknown whether we will stand in a saving relationship to Christ. When He foresees that this will be the case, He determines to save us on the basis of this foreknowledge. We are predestined to salvation on the basis of God's foreknowledge of our relationship to Christ. "For those whom He foreknew, He also predestined to become conformed to the image of His Son" (Romans 8:29).

The Son of God stands with arms outstretched and cries out, "Jerusalem, Jerusalem, who kills the prophets and stones those who are sent to her! How often I wanted to gather your children together, the way a hen gathers her chicks under her wings, and you were unwilling" (Matthew 23:37). But who IS willing? Who will humbly say, "Be gracious to me, O God, be gracious to me, for my soul takes refuge in You; and in the shadow of Your wings I will take refuge" (Psalms 57:1)? Who will flee to that Man who is "a refuge from the wind and a shelter from the storm, like streams of water in a dry country, like the shade of a huge rock in a parched land" (Isaiah 32:2)? Who will put on the Lord Jesus Christ, and let his life be hid with Christ in God (Romans 13:14; Colossians 3:3)? Who will identify himself with the lowly Servant who died for our sins? These are the ones whom the Father has already predestined to eternal life, based on His foreknowledge of our future saving relationship with Christ.

The question now is, *how* do we enter this relationship with Christ? Does God simply decide on His own which individuals He wants to be in heaven with Him for eternity, and then unilaterally change their hearts and transfer them into this eternal relationship with His Son—while leaving the rest to die in their sins? Or does God say to sinful mankind, "I want every single one of you to turn to Me and receive my salvation, but here are the few conditions you must meet before this transfer can be completed." The answer is the latter. Election (i.e., being chosen for eternal life in heaven) is conditional. God lays down certain conditions we must meet in order to share eternity with Him, and He foreknows from eternity past who will and who will not meet those conditions.

What, then, are the conditions one must meet in this Christian era in order to be chosen in Christ? The best way to explain it is to use a concept employed by the Apostle Paul to Mark the difference between those who are saved and those who are not, namely, *obedience to the gospel.* Paul refers to this twice when talking about salvation. In Romans 10:16 he refers to his physical Jewish kinfolk who are lost and declares, "But they have not all obeyed the gospel." In 2 Thessalonians 1:8 he says that when Jesus returns he will inflict vengeance "on those who do not obey the gospel of our Lord Jesus." If those who do not obey the gospel are lost, this implies that one must obey the gospel in order to be saved.

What does it mean, to "obey the gospel"? Obedience is how we are supposed to respond to commands. Most of God's commands are *law* commands, and our response to law commands is called "works of law" (see Romans 3:20, 28). But some of God's commands are instructions on how to receive salvation; these are *gospel* commands, and when we obey them we are "obeying the gospel." These gospel commands are the time-honored "plan of salvation" (at least, most of it): believe in Jesus, repent of sins, confess Jesus as Lord, and be buried with Him in baptism. These are the *conditions* a sinner must meet in order to receive salvation for the first time, and must continue to meet throughout his or her lifetime in order to stay saved. These are the conditions for entering into and staying in a saving relationship with Jesus Christ, the Chosen One.

How does this relate to election (i.e., predestination)? Remember Romans 8:29, "For those whom he foreknew he also predestined to be conformed to the image of his Son." The key word is "foreknew." Let's imagine for a moment that God has no foreknowledge. How then would He determine whether an individual would be saved or not? In such a case we would have to say that His final decision would be based on His observation of that person's lifetime as it passes, in order to verify "with His own eyes" whether that person meets the condition of lifelong obedience to the gospel. In this case the person's salvation is conditional, and God's decision to save is conditional, *post facto*.

But the reality is that God DOES have foreknowledge! Thus He does not have to wait for a person to live his or her life to its end to know whether or not that person will obey the gospel. He knows everything about every person's lifetime *before* it happens, from eternity past. Thus He knows if Joe X will obey the gospel or not; and on that basis, if His foreknowledge shows that Joe X will indeed obey the gospel, then God in eternity past predestines Joe X to heaven.

In summary, God, on the basis of His foreknowledge of our obedience to the gospel as the condition for our saving union with Christ, even before creation predestined that we shall be saved.

II. OBJECTIONS TO CONDITIONAL ELECTION

We shall now consider a few objections to the doctrine of conditional election. Some object first of all that God's foreknowledge is not really foreseeing but a kind of "foreloving." We can respond to this by saying simply that both are involved. To be foreseen *in Christ* IS to be *foreloved*. On a more technical level, though, we must say that the attempt to convert "foreknow" into "forelove" cannot pass the etymological test. I have discussed this in minute detail in my commentary on Romans, and will not go into the detail here. (See *The College Press NIV Commentary: Romans, Volume I*, 1996, pp. 502-511.)

Some object that God's foreknowledge of obedience to the gospel, especially the choice to believe (i.e., believe the gospel—Mark 1:15), does not solve any problem, since (in their view) faith itself is the gift of God, and God unconditionally chooses those to whom He will give it. We answer that there is no real evidence from Scripture to say that saving faith is the gift of God. Ephesians 2:8 is usually cited as part of the proof of this idea: "For by grace you have been saved through faith. And **this** is not your own doing; **it** is the gift of God." The contention is that the "this" and the "it" in this statement refer to faith and clearly declare it to be the gift of God. The fact is, however, that only one of these pronouns ("this") is in the original text; there is no word for "it" in the Greek. Also, the Greek pronoun "this" is neuter in gender, while the word for "faith" (*pistis*) is feminine in gender. Hence according to the rules of grammar, the gift cannot be faith since the genders do not match, but must be the general and inclusive concept of salvation.

Some object that if there is any condition whatsoever which the sinner has to meet, then God's sovereignty and freedom in salvation are destroyed, and He is made to depend upon man. We answer that God is the one who created the kind of world in which He knew sin and salvation could take place (i.e., a free-will universe), and He is the one who determined that sinners would receive salvation conditionally. And He is the one who established the conditions involved in obedience to the gospel. In making all these decisions, He was free to do it or not. He was in no way dependent upon human beings when He stipulated the gospel conditions. He sovereignly and freely set all this up to begin with.

III. CONDITIONAL ELECTION AND HUMAN RESPONSIBILITY

A few comments must be made about conditional election and human responsibility. First, conditional election respects man's ability to come to his own decision to believe in Christ and obey the gospel. What is really at stake here is the doctrine of total depravity, which denies that man can make his own decision and therefore requires that God make it for him. Total depravity makes it necessary for God to do the choosing unconditionally and unilaterally. Only when we rightly reject total depravity can we preserve human responsibility in the Acts of obeying the gospel.

Second, conditional election makes the blame rest solely upon man if he does not meet the conditions for salvation. It relieves God of that awful stigma of somehow being arbitrary and unjust for choosing some and leaving others behind.

Third, conditional election forces the unbeliever to face the problem of his own destiny squarely and without excuse. He cannot say, "What's the use? My fate is sealed anyway." Unconditional election is not supposed to engender this attitude, although it often does.

Finally, conditional election warns the believer that he must give diligence to make his calling and election sure. The ability to meet the conditions for election implies the ability to repudiate it at a later time. In other words, only those who persevere in faith to the end are truly elect. We must not shrink back and become destroyed, but must have faith and preserve our souls (Hebrews 10:39). Christ has reconciled us in His body of flesh through death, in order to present us holy and blameless before Him, IF indeed we continue in the faith, stable and steadfast, not shifting from the hope of the gospel that we heard (Colossians 1:22-23). "For if God did not spare the natural branches, neither will he spare you. Note then the kindness and the severity of God: severity toward those who have fallen, but God's kindness to you, provided you continue in his kindness. Otherwise you too will be cut off" (Romans 11:21-22).

IV. CONDITIONAL ELECTION AND ASSURANCE

Our final thoughts are about conditional election and the assurance of salvation. The proponents of unconditional election point out that such a notion as theirs is a great comfort to God's elect. To know that our salvation in no way depends on our own sinful and fickle selves, but wholly upon the gracious and sovereign God, is supposed to give the believer great peace of mind.

Ideally it should, and in fact it no doubt causes many to feel comforted about their salvation, whether it is warranted or not. But it is also true that the idea of unconditional election has been the source of great anguish to many. "Since I can do nothing but wait," they say (even if the doctrine itself may not warrant it), "how can I really be sure God has chosen me?" If the conditions for choosing one person and not another lie wholly within the secret counsels of God, a person may *always* wonder whether those conditions apply to him or not.

Conditional election, despite the possibility that a believer may fall away and lose his salvation, is a source of great comfort. How can one be assured that he is among God's elect? Because God has shown us what the conditions are for achieving this status, and every man and woman can know whether they have met these conditions or not. There is no mystery.

You know whether you are a baptized believer or not. If you are not, then be warned that the doctrine of predestination is not intended to be a comfort for unbelievers. If you are, then you can really mean it when you sing, "Blessed assurance, Jesus is mine; O what a foretaste of glory divine!"

This is an edited version of an essay originally published in *The Seminary Review*, a periodical of The Cincinnati Bible Seminary, vol. XII:4, Summer 1966, pp. 57-63. It was originally presented as part of a panel discussion on "Problem Passages in Ephesians" at the 1965 Conference on Evangelism, sponsored by CBS.

THE PREDESTINATION OF INDIVIDUALS

In the debate between Calvinism and non-Calvinism, the subject of predestination is often the center of attention. Calvinists interpret the Biblical teaching on predestination as saying that God has unconditionally and unilaterally predestined certain individuals to become believers and receive eternal life, while consigning all other individuals to eternal damnation. Non-Calvinists say that the relevant Biblical texts do not teach this at all. The fact is, though, that several key texts DO teach predestination to salvation. So how do non-Calvinists interpret these texts?

I have defended the most common non-Calvinist approach in several places, including chapter 22 of my book, *The Faith Once for All* (College Press, 2002), and including my chapter on "The Classical Arminian View of Election" in Chad Brand, ed., *Perspectives on Election: Five Views* (Broadman & Holman, 2006). This view is summed up as conditional election based on foreknowledge. (See the previous chapter in this book.)

Once in a while, though, another approach is followed by non-Calvinists in their attempt to refute the Calvinist view. They defend a view called corporate or group predestination. The idea here is that God predestines a particular group or category of people to heaven, without determining which individuals will be a part of that group. To say that God has predestined some people to salvation means only that He has said something like this: "Whoever believes in Jesus or whoever obeys the gospel will be in heaven for eternity." A popular way of summing up this view is this: "God predestines the plan, not the man."

The view presented by Robert Shank in his book *Elect in the Son* (Westcott 1970) basically takes this approach, as does an article by Donald Nash entitled "The Predetermined Plan" (*Christian Standard*, 9/12/1970, p. 10). Nash clearly affirms that God has predestined an impersonal group, rather than specific individuals, to eternal life.

In this essay I intend to show that this group-predestination view, however well-intentioned, is false. It is admirable to desire to refute Calvinism and to offer an alternative to Calvinistic predestination, but this is not a valid alternative. One creates a false dilemma by implying that we must choose either Calvinistic predestination or group predestination. It is certainly true that Calvinists teach individual predestination, but this is not what makes it Calvinistic. The distinctive element in Calvinistic predestination is not that *individuals* are predestined either to heaven or to hell, but that they are thus predestined *unconditionally*.

For example, the classic statement of Calvinism, the Westminster Confession of Faith (III.5), seems to speak of the predestined not as individuals but as a group when it refers to "Those of mankind that are predestinated unto life." But its real point is in what follows, when the Confession goes on to say that God has predestined this group "unto everlasting glory, out of his mere free grace and love, without any foresight of faith or good works, or perseverance in either of them, or any other thing in the creation, as conditions, or causes moving him thereunto." All Calvinists certainly see predestination as applying to individuals, but the key phrase here is "without … conditions."

I have attempted to refute the idea of *unconditional* election in other places (see the second paragraph in this essay, above). In this brief essay I will attempt to show why the idea of group or *corporate* predestination is also wrong. Biblical predestination (i.e., election) is conditional and individual.

I.   THE DOGMATIC PRESUPPOSITION

I will first examine one of the arguments against individual election and point out that it is not the result of sound exegesis but is actually just a dogmatic presupposition. This is the idea that individual election would be a denial of free will. For instance, after Brother Donald Nash gives his explanation of Romans 8:28-29, he says that now "we can see the verses do not teach that God predestined every individual's eternal destiny before time began without any possibility of free will on his part." However, the last part of that statement—about free will—is just added at this point and has not been established by any exegesis. It seems that it has already been decided that individual predestination is incompatible with free will and therefore must be rejected if free will is to be preserved.

The dogmatic argument against individual predestination thus seems to take this form: (a) If individuals are predestined, there can be no free will. (b) There is free will. (c) Therefore there can be no individual election. Now, this is good logic, and it would be good doctrine if the premises were valid. But unfortunately the major premise, (a) above, is not valid. Free will is perfectly compatible with individual predestination, for Romans 8:29 explicitly states that it is our final glorification that is predestined, not our free-will choices.

The key idea here is not *who* is predestined (groups or individuals), but what we are predestined *to*. Calvinists say the chosen are predestined *to believe*, to become believers, without themselves making any positive choice in the matter. This is indeed a denial of free will; Calvinists see all sinners as totally depraved as a result of Adam's sin, and thus totally unable to come to faith on their own. There is no free will choice involved in their coming to faith.

However, in Romans 8:29 Paul does not say anyone is predestined to become a believer; he says we are "predestined to be conformed to the image of his Son, in order that he might be the firstborn among many brothers." All of this language shows he is talking about the resurrection of the believer's body into a glorious body like that of Jesus (Philippians

3:21), which fulfills our adoption into the family of God (Romans 8:23). This bodily resurrection makes us siblings of Jesus, the firstborn from the dead (Colossians 1:18); after this event of predestined resurrection is finally accomplished, He is "the firstborn among many brothers." This is definitely NOT a predestination to faith, which is indeed our free-will choice; it is a predestination to something we have no part in, i.e., our bodily resurrection into eternal life.

The challenge to free will does not come from the idea of individual election, but from unconditional election. That fact that free will is not ruled out by individual election but is compatible with it—i.e., that free will is actually presupposed by individual predestination—is seen in the reference to foreknowledge, which is God's foreknowledge of free-will choices that we will make in response to conditions God has set for receiving salvation. God knows these choices beforehand, and He knows the persons whom He predestinates. What does He know about them? He knows "before the foundation of the world" (Ephesians 1:4) which individuals will freely choose to meet the gospel conditions for being saved, and will thus enter into a saving union with Jesus Christ. The Bible makes it clear that we enter this union through our own acts, namely, believing, repenting, confessing, and being baptized.

II. THE EXEGETICAL ARGUMENT

Now I will show the fallacy of another argument for group election. In seeking to argue against individual predestination from the text in Romans 8:29, Donald Nash focuses upon the word "whom," in the sentence, "For those WHOM he foreknew he also predestined." Nash says, "But the word 'whom' is not singular and is not speaking of specific individuals. It is plural in the original language and is speaking of a group or class of people."

This is a strange argument, because it simply does not follow that a plural pronoun must always refer to an impersonal class rather than to several individuals considered as individuals. If we were to adopt such a rule and infer "group" wherever there is a plural pronoun, we would succeed in depersonalizing most of the promises and commandments of Scripture. (Consider, for example, 2 Timothy 2:19, "The Lord knows those who are his." Here "those" is the plural pronoun *tous*. Does the plural mean that He knows only the group and not the individuals in the group? The answer is obvious.)

Besides this, there are two expressions which are very well suited for use in referring to an impersonal group or class of persons. One occurs in this very chapter, in Romans 8:14, "For all who are led by the Spirit of God are sons of God." The Greek word translated "all" is *hosoi* (masculine plural of *hosos*), which literally means "whoever, as many as." (See also Romans 6:3.) The other such term, *hostis*, is often used generically or to designate persons or things belonging to a certain class; it is translated by such expressions as "whoever" or "everyone who," especially in Jesus's teaching (e.g., Matthew 5:39; 10:32). Neither of these expressions appears in Romans 8:29, however, where we would expect such a pronoun if group predestination were the point. Instead, the plural form of the ordinary relative pronoun (*hous*) is used, referring to many individuals.

One could perhaps argue that if a group were intended here, this idea could easily be expressed by a singular pronoun referring to a particular type of individual and not to any particular individual. In fact, the argument would probably be more convincing if such a singular pronoun were used (e.g., *hos*, often translated "whoever"). But such language is not used.

The questions still remains, are there positive reasons for believing that God predestines *individuals* to salvation? To this question we now turn.

III. THE NATURE OF GOD

The first argument for individual predestination is that nothing else is worthy of the nature of God. God is infinite, which simply means unlimited. His infinity includes His knowledge, which means that His knowledge is unlimited—He is omniscient. He is also infinite with regard to time, which means He is not limited by the passing of time the way created beings are. This means two things. One, it means that when we consider time as a linear succession of moments with a "before" and a "now" and an "after," God is infinite in both directions. He has existed before now into infinite past time (i.e., eternity past) without having a beginning, and He will by nature exist after now into infinite future time (i.e., eternity future) without ever ending. "From everlasting to everlasting, you are God" (Psalms 90:2).

In the second place, God's eternity is not just a quantitative distinction between Him and His creation. God's eternity is also qualitatively different from everything else. That God is eternal means that He is not bound by the restrictions of time in the way creatures are. There is a real sense in which He is above time, or outside of time. This is not true in an absolute sense, though. I believe time in the sense of existing along a time line—experiencing the now, remembering the past, and expecting the future—is part of God's essence. He is not completely "timeless," contrary to what many have assumed. (See my essay, "Understanding God: God and Time," which is chapter 3 in William Baker, ed., *Evangelicalism and the Stone-Campbell Movement, Vol. 2: Engaging Basic Christian Doctrine* [ACU Press, 2006].)

In what sense, then, is God above or outside time? According to Biblical teaching, God's *knowledge* is not limited by time. At any given moment, what is both past and future to us, and even to God in terms of his existence and experience, is present in God's knowledge or consciousness. He always knows the events that have occurred and will occur over the entire scope of time, as if it were all a panorama of "the now." This is the sense in which the great "I AM" transcends time: He sees it all from beginning to end at one and the same moment. This is how He is able to prophesy future events; see the many references to this in Isaiah 40-48.

It is only on the basis of this aspect of God's nature that we can understand His *foreknowledge*, which is crucial to his predestination of individuals to salvation. Certainly God foreknows; He cannot help but foreknow, just because He is God. So when Romans 8:29 and 1 Peter 1:1-2 say that God foreknows and therefore predestines, we must be very careful not to emasculate this foreknowledge by saying that this word does not really mean that God actually *knows* something beforehand, as Calvinists attempt to do. To say that God could not foreknow free human decisions is either to exalt man too highly or to reduce God to creaturely status.

God sees the entire scope of every individual's lifetime long before it flashes on the screen of history. He knows what free-will choices every human being will make. On the basis of this foreknowledge He can and does determine every individual's final destiny even before the foundation of the world.

The point is this. If God's foreknowledge is real, and if it is really *foreknowledge*, and if He predestines on the basis of this foreknowledge, then His predestining must be the predestination of *individuals*. To say that he "foreknows" just a plan or some unpopulated group is nonsense. The nature and reality of foreknowledge is simply inconsistent with this whole idea.

IV. THE BIBLICAL TEACHING ABOUT PREDESTINATION

The final point is that the Bible clearly teaches that God sometimes elects or predestines certain *individuals* to specific ends. This becomes obvious when we analyze the various types of predestination mentioned in the Bible. From the standpoint of the goal or end to which someone is predestined, that goal may be salvation or even damnation, or simply a particular office or task. From the standpoint of the ones who are predestined, they may be chosen either as groups or as individuals.

The fact is that there is a kind of group predestination, illustrated in God's choosing the nation of Israel for a specific role of service. The Israelites as a nation were chosen for the task of preparing for the incarnation of God the Logos in the role of Savior of the world (Genesis 12:1-3; Deuteronomy 7:6-8; Isaiah 44:1; see Romans 11:2).

More often, however, God's predestination is directed toward individuals. This is not always a predestination to salvation; sometimes it is a predestination to service. God chose and predestined many individuals to fulfill certain roles or tasks in relation to His eternal purpose of salvation. For example, He chose certain particular rulers for their roles. He raised up the Pharaoh of the Exodus (Romans 9:17). He called Cyrus by name more than two centuries before he was born, and appointed him to be His own "shepherd" (Isaiah 44:28 — 45:6).

Some prophets and apostles likewise were specifically predestined as individuals to perform their tasks. The Lord told Jeremiah, "Before I formed you in the womb I knew you, and before you were born I consecrated you; I appointed you a prophet to the nations" (Jeremiah 1:5). The twelve apostles were chosen to fill their roles; even Judas's role was determined beforehand (John 6:70; 17:12; Acts 2:23). God had already determined who was to be the "apostle to the Gentiles" even from that individual's birth (Galatians 1:15; Acts 9:15).

The outstanding example of individual predestination, of course, is the predestination of Jesus Christ to perform the work of salvation. He is the Servant chosen from the foundation of the world (Isaiah 42:1; 1 Peter 1:20). What happened to Jesus was foreknown and predestined (Acts 2:23; 4:28).

We should not be surprised, then, to find clear passages of Scripture which teach individual predestination to salvation. First Peter 1:1-2 presents precisely the same teaching that is found in Romans 8:29, namely, predestination to salvation based on foreknowledge. And in Peter's case it is obvious that he is not speaking of a class of individuals, but of specific individuals who were living in a specific area of the world at that time: the "elect exiles of the dispersion in Pontus, Galatia, Cappadocia, Asia, and Bithynia."

In 2 Thessalonians 2:13 Paul reminds the Thessalonian Christians that "God chose you as the first fruits to be saved, through sanctification by the Spirit and belief in the truth."

A third reference should end the discussion. Revelation 17:8 refers to those "whose names have not been written in the book of life from the foundation of the world." This is a negative statement; but if there are some people whose names have *not* been written in the book of life, then there are some whose names *have* been written there from the beginning.

Rejoice that your names are thus written in heaven (Luke 10:20)!

GOD'S FOREKNOWLEDGE: WHY IS IT IMPORTANT?

QUESTION: Does the Bible teach that God knows the future? How important is it that we understand this doctrine?

ANSWER: This is the question of divine *foreknowledge*. One of the main attributes of God is called "omniscience," which literally means the knowledge of everything. As usually applied, to say that God is omniscient means that He knows everything. This means He knows all possibilities as well as all actualities. In the category of actualities, this means He has complete knowledge of the actual past, the actual present, and the actual future. His knowledge of the future is His foreknowledge.

Divine foreknowledge has always been accepted by most Bible-believers. There have been different explanations of it, however. The usual view is that God knows the future simply because He is infinite (unlimited) in nature and is thus not limited by time. Calvinists, though, deny that God can literally see into the future. Nevertheless, they believe that God knows what is going to happen in the future because they believe He has *predetermined* everything (literally, *everything*) that will ever happen. Thus His knowledge of the future is not a real "foreknowledge," but simply the knowledge of what He Himself has planned to do as the future unfolds. This is how He knows what human beings will do in the future. They do not have genuine free will; they will do only what God has foreordained them to do, and which He thus "foreknows" that they will do.

In recent times some have taken to denying foreknowledge altogether. This denial is found mainly in the fairly recent theological movement (1980s &ff.) known as "openness theology" or "openness theism." Influential representatives include Richard Rice, Clark Pinnock, John Sanders, and Greg Boyd. This view affirms that God cannot know the future, simply because there IS no future to be known. God is still omniscient because he knows everything there is to know; he is not expected to know actualities that do not yet exist. One of the main points of this view is the claim that if God did know the future, there could be no free will. Everything, including every human decision, would be set in stone by the very fact that God foreknows it; thus no one would be free to choose otherwise.

In this brief essay I will show that the Bible DOES in fact teach that God foreknows everything about the future of His creation. I will show that such foreknowledge is very important for some of the most significant elements of the Biblical world view. (It is just serendipitous that all four points are alliterative—all begin with "Pr—".)

I.   PROPHECY.

Generic prophecy is by definition any message spoken on behalf of someone else. One major kind of prophecy, though, is *predictive* prophecy, i.e., a message that predicts something that is going to happen in the future. The Bible has many examples where God predicts future events, often things that will happen hundreds of years later. Some of these can be explained by God's purposive plan to personally cause an event to happen at a chosen point in the future, especially predictions relating to the birth of the Messiah (e.g., Isaiah 7:14).

Some predictive prophecies, though, are the result of God's foreknowledge of as-yet-future human free-will choices, i.e., choices that he knows certain people will make in certain circumstances yet in the future. One such prophecy is Isaiah 44:28: "It is I who says of Cyrus, 'He is My shepherd! And he will perform all My desire.' And he declares of Jerusalem, 'She will be built.' And of the temple, 'Your foundation will be laid.'" This prophecy was written probably in the late eighth century B.C., about the man who became king of Persia almost 200 years later (c. 539 B.C.). The fulfillment of this and other prophecies related to Cyrus is recorded in the book of Ezra (see Ezra 1:1-4). King Cyrus defeated the Babylonians, set the Judean captives free, and allowed them to return to their homeland to rebuild Jerusalem and the temple.

Another predictive prophecy involving God's foreknowledge of future human Acts is Psalms 22:17-18, "I can count all my bones. They look, they stare at me; they divide my garments among them. And for my clothing they cast lots." This is a Psalm of David, whose life ended around 970 B.C. Thus it refers to something that was going to happen a thousand years later (Matthew 27:35-36), something foreknown to God and revealed to David by the Holy Spirit. For another example see Jesus' own prediction concerning the Apostle Peter, made during the Last Supper, the night before the crucifixion: "Truly I say to you, that this very night, before a rooster crows twice, you yourself will deny Me three times" (Mark 14:30). The amount of detail here shows that this was not a guess, but a predictive prophecy based on foreknowledge.

These are just two examples of prophecies related to the events connected with Christ's death. We should not be surprised that such prophecies exist, since the Apostle Peter affirms that everything related to this atoning death was either planned by or foreknown to God. In Acts 2:23 he says that Jesus was "delivered up according to the definite plan and foreknowledge of God." The death of Christ was definitely a plan God had predetermined to accomplish from all eternity (Revelation 13:8, NIV; see 1 Peter 1:20), but it involved using many free-will decisions that God *knew in advance* and included in this plan. These included Judas' betrayal, Herod's and Pilate's decisions, the Jews' rejection of Jesus, and Jesus's execution by the Romans (see Acts 2:23b; 4:27-28). God wove together the threads of His own blessed plan of redemption and the threads of the foreknown free Acts of unbelievers, and produced a tapestry of unbelievable harmony and eternal significance.

II. PROOF.

The second example of the importance of foreknowledge is actually a continuation of the first one. It is simply this: the fact that God foreknows the future, as demonstrated by His predictive prophecies, PROVES that He alone is God. There are always many false gods whose reality and deity and power are claimed by their followers. To such claims the One True God says: "OK, if you are a god, *prove it!* And one main way you can prove it is to *predict the future!* These phony gods cannot do this, BUT I CAN DO IT, AND I HAVE DONE IT! My unique foreknowledge of the future *proves* that I alone am God!" In other words, the very Mark of deity is the ability to declare what is going to take place in the future, the ability to announce what is coming.

Several times in Isaiah 40-48 God issues this challenge to His so-called rivals. For example, in 44:7-8 He says, "'Who is like Me? Let him proclaim and declare it; yes, let him recount it to Me in order, from the time that I established the ancient nation. And let them declare to them the things that are coming and the events that are going to take place. Do not tremble and do not be afraid; have I not long since announced it to you and declared it? And you are My witnesses. Is there any God besides Me, or is there any other Rock? I know of none.'"

Another such example is 45:20-21: "'Gather yourselves and come; draw near together, you fugitives of the nations; they have no knowledge, who carry about their wooden idol and pray to a god who cannot save. Declare and set forth your case; indeed, let them consult together. Who has announced this from of old? Who has long since declared it? Is it not I, the Lord? And there is no other God besides Me, a righteous God and a Savior; there is none except Me.'"

For one more example see Isaiah 41:21-23, "Set forth your case, says the LORD; bring your proofs, says the King of Jacob. Let them bring them, and tell us what is to happen. Tell us the former things, what they are, that we may consider them, that we may know their outcome; or declare to us the things to come. Tell us what is to come hereafter, that we may know that you are gods." See also Isaiah 42:8-9; 46:9-10; 48:3-7. In all these passages God asserts His exclusive possession of knowledge of the future. Such foreknowledge, He says, is proof that He and He alone is the One True God.

III. PRAYER.

Some have concluded that if prayer is meaningful, then it must have the power to change God's mind. But this seems to somehow make God's will depend on ours. How can we say that God answers prayers without somehow diminishing the nature of God? (I discuss this in my book on *God the Ruler*, pp. 367ff.)

The answer lies in the foreknowledge of God. Even before He created this universe, He already knew every prayer that would ever be uttered. Even then He was able to decide which prayers He would answer and how He would answer them. Thus there is no need for God to change His plans in response to our petitions. From the beginning He has known them, and has known what He has planned to do about them. Answers to prayers are prearranged according to foreknowledge.

This is how C. S. Lewis saw it. Even though we may pray for a healing today, said Lewis, if God in eternity decided to grant it, He has already set in motion the causes necessary for its accomplishment. "Our prayers, and other free acts, are known to us only as we come to the moment of doing them. But they are eternally in the score of the great symphony" (Lewis, *Letters to Malcolm*, 1964, p. 69).

This shows that even though our prayers do not change God's mind, they do *influence* what God decides to do. In his foreknowledge, as God processes all our foreseen Acts and decisions—including our prayers, He plans His own decisions and deeds in connection with them. Thus some of the things God has determined to do, in answer to our prayers, He would never have done if we had not uttered these (foreknown) prayers!

IV. PREDESTINATION.

The final reason why foreknowledge is important is the one Paul is emphasizing in Romans 8:29, namely, that God's foreknowledge of our free choices is the means by which He predestines us to be part of His eternal family in heaven: "For those whom He foreknew, He also predestined to become conformed to the image of His Son, so that He would be the firstborn among many brethren."

Some Christians do not like to talk or think about predestination, because they associate it with Calvinism. But there is a huge difference between how Calvinists understand predestination, and the predestination to which Paul is referring here. Both sides correctly define predestination as God's pre-creation decision to later bestow salvation on some people and not others. Both sides correctly believe that God is the one who chooses whom to save and whom not to save.

But here is where the similarity ends. There are at least two HUGE differences between Calvinistic predestination and the predestination to which Paul refers in Romans 8:29. One difference focuses on the CONTENT of the salvation God predetermines to bestow on His chosen ones. Paul specifies that God predestines that we (the chosen ones) will be "conformed to the image of His Son." The context of Romans 8 shows that he is speaking specifically of the fact that God will give us, in the end times, a new, glorified, resurrection body just like the one Jesus has now (vv. 11, 18-23; cf. Philippians 3:21). This is when we will be fully adopted into God's family (vv. 15-17, 19, 22-23). This is why verse 29 refers to Jesus as "the firstborn among many brethren": He was the "*first*born from the dead" (Colossians 1:18), but not the only one. God has already predestined that we too will be "reborn from the dead," i.e., raised in new bodies into God's eternal family.

But how does Calvinism interpret the salvation to which certain people are predestined? They do not limit it as Paul does here, but affirm instead that God has predestined to bestow upon certain chosen ones *the entire scope of salvation*, beginning with the act of faith itself. He chooses not just who will be in heaven in the end, but who (of all the sinners in the world) will *become believers* and *remain believers* until they die and are raised again. But this is not what Paul says! Paul says only the END is predestined, not the MEANS. Calvinists incorrectly say both. They are wrong.

This leads to the other main difference between Calvinist and Biblical predestination. It has to do with the REASON why God chooses and predestines some, but not others. How does God decide whom to predestine to heaven? Here is where the word and concept of *foreknowledge* become important! Paul says that the ones God FOREKNOWS are the ones He predestines. Exactly what does He *foreknow* about us that causes Him to choose us? In a nutshell, He foreknows *who will meet the conditions for salvation that He specifies* at any point in redemptive history.

It is Calvinists themselves who introduce this concept of conditions into the discussion. The Calvinist system of sin and salvation is usually summarized in the acrostic T-U-L-I-P. The "T" is *total depravity*, which is actually why God has to choose who will believe and who will not: every human being is born (because of Adam) with a sinful nature that is so severe that no one is able to believe, or to meet any other conditions that God might specify for receiving eternal life. Therefore God's choice of certain ones has nothing to do with a "foreknowledge" of who will meet specified conditions, such as faith and repentance. Thus they speak of the "U" of *unconditional election*, where true foreknowledge is irrelevant.

But Paul says the predestination to heaven is somehow based on God's foreknowledge of something about us, and we conclude from other Biblical texts that this is a foreknowledge of *who will indeed* meet the *conditions* God has specified for receiving salvation. We think of these conditions as the "gospel commands" of believe, repent, confess, and be baptized. Thus because God foreknows from the beginning who will obey the gospel, He can predestine who will receive the final gift of a renewed and glorified body just like the one Jesus has now. (This is the "purpose" according to which we have been "called"; see v. 28.)

(For more details on predestination, see chapter 22 in my book *The Faith Once for All*; and my essay on "The Classical Arminian View of Election," in the book edited by Chad Brand, *Perspectives on Election: Five Views*; Broadman & Holman, 2006.)

Here, then, are four reasons why the reality of God's foreknowledge is important for our Christian living and thinking. It is a key presupposition of certain PROPHECIES; it is a solid PROOF of God's unique existence; it is a factor in our PRAYER life; and it is the basis for our PREDESTINATION to heaven. Other specific references to foreknowledge are as follows: God foreknew His people Israel (Romans 11:2), and He foresaw the justification of the Gentiles (Galatians 3:8). See also David's remarkable claims (Psalms 139:4, 16). The fact that names have been written in the Lamb's Book of Life from the foundation of the world is a clear indication of God's foreknowledge (Revelation 13:8; 17:8). Thus to deny divine foreknowledge requires one to either ignore a large portion of Scripture, or else undertake the major and futile task of trying to explain all these texts away.

IS EVERYTHING "GOD'S WILL"?

QUESTION: Our pastor says that everything is God's will. Is this true? How can we understand "God's will"?

ANSWER: People mean different things when they use language like this. I could say, "Whatever happens is the will of God," and it would be true because I am using the phrase "will of God" in the Biblical sense. However, when a Calvinist says the very same thing—"Whatever happens is the will of God"—his statement is false, because he does not MEAN the same thing that I mean, and therefore it would not be Biblical. You see, Calvinism has a false and unbiblical understanding of the language of God's will. So—to know what your "pastor" means when he says that "everything is God's will," I would have to know if he is a Calvinist or not—or if he has just picked up some Calvinist ideas without realizing it. Let me explain.

The New Testament words for "will," as used in the context of "God's will," can mean one of three things: God's desire, God's purpose, or God's permission. In view of this variety of connotations, it is indeed correct to say, EVERYTHING THAT HAPPENS IS THE WILL OF GOD. But two different people can make this same assertion, and mean two entirely different things by it, depending on which of these three categories they have in mind.

We should note that this statement ("everything that happens is the will of God") applies only to things that fall into one of the last two categories of the three things that constitute God's will. Things to which "God's purpose" and "God's permission" apply will always be things that actually happen. The phrase "God's desire" refers to things He *wants* to happen, but they may or may not actually happen. If these desired things *also* fall into the category of "God's purpose," they will actually happen. Coming from another direction, some things that actually happen will not be what God desires. These would be some of the things that fall under the heading of "God's permission," because things in this category may or may not also be "God's desire." Sometimes He *permits* things to happen that He does not personally desire (such as sinful acts), and sometimes the things that He desires do not actually happen (such as universal salvation). What makes this so complicated is the fact that human beings have free will, and whether some things happen or not depends on human free-will choices.

Now, we shall examine the right and wrong meanings of the statement, "Everything that happens is the will of God." First, when a Calvinist makes this statement, he means that *everything* that happens is God's will in BOTH of the first two senses if the word *will*, namely, "desire" and "purpose." In Calvinism, whatever happens is both desired and caused by God.

The fundamental element in the Calvinist world view is the concept of an "eternal decree." I.e., before anything else happens, God draws up in His mind a detailed, meticulous blueprint that includes everything that will ever happen within the creation He is about to bring into existence. In this sense the blueprint is comprehensive. Also, everything in the blueprint (decree), whether in the realm of nature or in the realm of human actions, is there by God's sole choice. Every detail originates in the mind of God. He is the only one who has any say about it, any input into it. We human creatures have *nothing* to do with its content; the decree is completely unconditioned by anything outside of God. Whatever is in the decree is there because God *wants* it to be there, period. This includes all human actions and apparent decisions. Thus everything that happens is the will of God in the sense that He *desires* it.

This eternal decree is also described as efficacious, or causative. I.e., whatever takes place in our world happens because it was in the decree, period. God put it there because he wants it to happen; and because He wants it to happen, it is His eternal purpose to *make* it happen. That is what world history is: God turning His eternal decree into reality. Thus everything that happens is the will of God in the sense that it is part of His PURPOSE (and it is His purpose because He desires it). And if it is His purpose, He will make sure that it happens. Whatever happens is desired by God, purposed by God, and in the end *caused* by God. Out of this system we get the common but erroneous belief that "everything happens for a reason," or "there's a purpose for everything."

As one Calvinist puts it, God has a "predetermined plan" for everything. "It is that which WILL HAPPEN. It is inevitable, unconditional, immutable, irresistible, comprehensive, and purposeful ... . It includes everything—even sin and suffering. It involves everything— even human responsibility and human decisions" (J. G. Howard, *Knowing God's Will*, Zondervan 1976, p. 12). Another Calvinist says that "the final answer to the question why a thing is and why it is as it is must ever remain: 'God willed it,' according to his absolute sovereignty" (H. Bavinck, *The Doctrine of God*, Eerdmans 1951, p. 371). I.e., whatever happens is the will of God, both in the sense of God's desire and in the sense of God's purpose.

In my judgment the above approach to "the will of God" is entirely and demonically false. SOME things happen because God desires and purposes them, but not everything. This is why it is especially important to know that the word "will" can also mean "permit, allow." When we understand this, we can truly say that EVERYTHING THAT HAPPENS IS THE WILL OF GOD, *but not in the same sense!*

Of course, God does decree or purpose some things to happen, especially things relating to creation and redemption. If He decrees or purposes something to happen, then He has already desired for it to happen and at the proper time He will cause it to happen. For example, God willed for "the heavens and the earth" to be created (Genesis 1:1), because He wanted them to exist. As the angelic beings declare in their worship of God, "You created all things, and by your will they existed and were created" (Revelation 4:11). This universe in its original form, including free-will beings, was God's desire and God's purpose. Another example of God's desiring and purposing something to happen is the cross of Jesus Christ. The Apostle Peter declares in Acts 2:23 that it was predetermined by God that Jesus would be "delivered up according to the definite plan and foreknowledge of God."

But because God created this world to be inhabited by free-will creatures, most things that happen in it are not *purposed* by God but rather *permitted* by Him. God desires us free-will creatures to do many things that we do not do (e.g., 2 Peter 3:9), and He desires us *not* to do many things that we do (commit sins, especially). Thus His will in the sense of "desire" does not always happen. But even in these kinds of cases, whatever happens does so *only* because God PERMITS it to happen.

James 4:13-15 clearly identifies this permissive aspect of the divine will: "Come now, you who say, 'Today or tomorrow we will go into such and such a town, and spend a year there and trade and make a profit.' Yet you do not know what tomorrow will bring. What is your life? For you are a mist that appears for a little time and then vanishes. Instead you ought to say, 'If the Lord wills, we will live and do this or that.'" Here, "if the Lord *wills*" means "if the Lord *permits*" in the same sense as Acts 18:21 and 1 Corinthians 4:19 (see Romans 1:10; 15:32; 1 Peter 4:19). The point is that God *could prevent* anything that is about to happen if He should choose to do so; and sometimes, according to His purposive will, He does just that (Luke 12:20).

But in most cases He wills to *allow* things to happen according to our own plans and choices, thus allowing our free choices to determine our own destinies. Nevertheless, God still has the final say, in this sense: even when things happen as the result of our own wills, He is "willing" them to happen in the sense that he is PERMITTING them to happen. (He could have prevented them if He so chose.) So even these things *are the will of God*—but *not* in the sense that He is purposing or causing them. They are the result of his *permissive* will only.

To sum up, "Everything that happens is *either* the purposive will of God *or* the permissive will of God." We must never forget this distinction between God *causing* something to happen and God's *allowing* it to happen. Also, "Only *some* things that happen are God's purposive will, and some things that happen are *not* God's purposive will." Only the Calvinist mentality puts *everything* under God's purposive will.

So—what does your "pastor" mean when he says that "everything is God's will"? If he means that God has decreed everything and is causing everything according to His own eternal purpose, this is not Biblical. It is the essence of Calvinism. But if he means that some things are God's will in the sense that he purposes and causes them, but other things are God's will only in the sense that He permits them, then he is correct. The latter is the Biblical view.

(Some Calvinists do use the terminology of God's "permissive" will. I.e., they will say that some things [usually sins] do happen only because of God's permissive will. This is deceptive, however, because in the Calvinist system true permission is incompatible with the eternal decree to which they are committed. When Calvinists appeal to divine "permission," they must always redefine it until it is meaningless or contradictory. More than once I have heard Calvinists use the expression "efficacious permission"—an obvious contradiction of terms. For more on this false concept of permission, see my essay, "The Nature of the Divine Sovereignty," in *The Grace of God, the Will of Man*, ed. Clark Pinnock [Zondervan, 1989], 105-106.)

For more details on the content of this study, see my book, *What the Bible Says about God the Ruler* (College Press; now, Wipf and Stock), chapter 8, "The Will of God" (pp. 299-329).

DOES GOD HAVE A PLAN FOR EVERY PERSON'S LIFE?

QUESTION: Have all the days of our lives already been planned or set by God? If God has "set" the days for our lives, does our free will change that? E.g, when a baby is aborted, does that change the days God had originally set for that life? When we abuse our own bodies (e.g., via smoking, drinking, over-eating), does that change the days He had set for us? Or has He somehow worked that into His plan?

ANSWER: It is very commonly believed that God does indeed have a set plan for each individual's life. There are two versions of this idea. One is the Calvinist view, which says that God from all eternity has already predetermined (predestined) "whatsoever comes to pass," including every detail of every person's life. We have no real choice in the matter. If there is an abortion, or if we harm our health through smoking or over-eating, that is simply part of what God has preordained will take place. That IS his "set plan," and whatever He has planned will infallibly occur.

J. G. Howard, in his book, *Knowing God's Will—and Doing It!* (Zondervan 1976), says it this way: "Scripture teaches us that God has a predetermined plan for every life. It is that which WILL HAPPEN. It is inevitable, unconditional, immutable, irresistible, comprehensive, and purposeful. It is also, for the most part, unpredictable. It includes everything—even sin and suffering. It involves everything—even human responsibility and human decisions" (p. 12). Even people who are not

Calvinists sometimes assume that something like this is true. We commonly hear things like: "Everything happens for a reason." "There's a purpose for everything." After the New Orleans Saints won the 2010 Super Bowl, winning quarterback Drew Brees exulted, "I'm just feeling like it was all meant to be."

This is simply not true. God has NOT predetermined everything that will happen. He created human beings with free will, and He tells us in His Word what choices He wants us to make. But He does not make our choices for us; that would go against His purpose to create free-will beings in the first place. He does not set or plan our days for us. Via His permissive will He allows us to make our own choices, even those that go against His commands and desires. Because of His omniscience God FOREKNOWS all the choices we will make with our free wills, and He pre-plans His own responses to these choices; but He does not cause us to do anything.

But did not David praise God that, while he was still in his mother's womb, "Thine eyes have seen my unformed substance; and in Thy book they were all written, the days that were ordained for me, when as yet there was not one of them" (Psalms 139:16)? Did God not say of Jeremiah, "Before I formed you in the womb I knew you, and before you were born I consecrated you; I have appointed you a prophet to the nations" (Jeremiah 1:5)? Did not Paul testify that God had set him apart, even from his mother's womb (Galatians 1:15)? Yes, through His foreknowledge and His providential intervention in the lives of these men (see Acts 2:23), God did indeed have a plan for them and a set purpose for their lives. But we should not presume that the same is true for every life; we have no warrant for universalizing these remarks that were made about certain specific individuals whom God prepared for special roles in His redemptive plan.

The second version of this idea that God has a set plan for each person's life says that God has an IDEAL plan all worked out for each individual, but He leaves it up to us to *discover* what that ideal plan is and to *implement* it ourselves. This applies to major decisions, such as our choice of spouse, or vocation, or college; and some think it applies to every decision we make every day, such as our choice of what to wear, what to eat for breakfast, and what route to take to work. Since God does not tell us what His plan for us is, many conscientious people agonize over whether they have made the right decisions or have missed out on God's will on a particular thing.

Though this is not as serious an error as Calvinism, it is still an erroneous approach to the question of whether or not we are conforming to God's "set plan" for our lives. Apart from the relatively few individuals in Bible history whom He selected for special roles in His redemptive plan, God does not actually have an individual, unique, specific "set plan" or "ideal plan" for each person. He has a GENERAL plan for all of us, as revealed in His inspired Word, the Bible. This plan is embodied in the law codes that apply in specific eras in history. His plan is for each of us to be holy, as He is holy (1 Peter 1:15-16). Our New Covenant law code tells us how to accomplish this. We call this His preceptive will, and it applies equally to everyone. His general plan for all of us also includes his desire that all would be saved (Matthew 23:37; 1 Timothy 2:4; 2 Peter 3:9).

Even though God WANTS all of us to do all these things, He does not cause us to do them. He leaves it up to our own initiative to study His Word and discover His commands and His desires for us, which are the same for everyone. He also leaves it up to our free-will choices as to whether we will conform our lives to His will in these matters.

But what about the decisions that are not directly covered by His revealed will, such as whom to marry and what vocation to pursue and what car to buy? Two comments are in order. First, in His preceptive will revealed in Scripture, there are *general principles* we are obligated to apply that are relevant to most decisions we will ever have to make. E.g., regarding marriage, God's Word teaches that we must keep sex within marriage, that marriage is between a man and a woman, and that Christians should marry Christians. Regarding what to cook for supper,

God's Word teaches that one should provide for his family (1 Timothy 5:8) and provide the food that will promote good health and life (and thus not break the sixth commandment).

My second comment is this. Though God has drawn some general boundaries that apply to most matters, as long as we stay within those boundaries, God *does not care* what specific choices we make. As long as we fulfill His general requirements for our lives, most of the specific decisions *do not matter*. God has no "set will" or "set plan" for the specific person we should marry, for example. As long as we stay under the umbrella of teachings such as those mentioned above, we may marry whomever we choose (and whoever will have us!).

(For a more complete discussion of this, see my book, *What the Bible Says About God the Ruler* [College Press, 1984], chapter 8 on "The Will of God.")

WHAT IS GOD DOING IN THE WORLD?

QUESTION: I hear a lot of ministers talking about "what God is doing in the world." They tell the church that God is "doing a great work" here or there, or that he is about to do some really great thing. How is this different from Calvinism? How do we know what God is or is not doing?

ANSWER: When I was a student at Princeton Theological Seminary in the late 1960s, I heard this language quite often, especially in connection with the work of the church and the work of missions. We were told to "look around you, and find out where God is working in the world, and then get on board with Him," i.e., join in and help Him accomplish what He has already begun.

Of course, in those days Princeton was quite liberal theologically, and one of the big liberal fads was liberation theology. The big concern of liberation theology was to "liberate" "oppressed" groups from captivity to patriarchalism, racial discrimination, and economic injustice. Capitalism especially was the Great Satan, and the heroes were the Marxist revolutionaries who were fighting to overthrow oppressive governments in areas such as Latin America. This is where God was identified as working. God was seen as using feminists and Marxist rebels to bring about the changes He desired, and we could be on God's side if we joined in these movements.

This segment of church history illustrates a common tendency among Christians, namely that whenever any of us sees a movement or circumstance going on in the world that we approve of, we assume and declare that "it must be from God." Among conservatives this is especially true if it is something happening in connection with the church or with Christendom in general.

We see this tendency especially in reference to church growth, usually defined in numerical terms. We are quite familiar with megachurch mania, where size and glory increase together. To be a megachurch (with average attendance exceeding 2,000 weekly) is seen as a sign that "God is at work" in that congregation. The *Christian Standard*'s 2018 list of such Christian Churches (Restoration Movement) included 55 congregations, with another 72 averaging 1,000 — 1,999 weekly. The largest listed church was Christ's Church of the Valley (Peoria AZ), averaging 28,216 in weekly attendance. Surely God must be at work among us, especially in those missional churches focusing on community service.

Are large numbers a sign that God is at work, that God is doing a great thing among us? If so, then He must *really* be busy among some other groups! In 2016 Southern Baptists had 47,272 congregations, according to Wikipedia, with 595 having a weekly attendance of 1,000 or more (compared to 127 such Christian Churches that are known). In 2014 the Second Baptist Church in the Houston area averaged 26,022 weekly attendance at its several campuses. (Joel Osteen's Lakewood Church in Houston draws over 45,000 each week, according to its 2017 website.)

But even these numbers are far surpassed by what many call the fastest-growing group of denominations in the world: the Pentecostal and Charismatic churches, or "renewalist movements" as some call them. Worldwide they encompass over half a billion followers. A book by Paul Alexander is titled *Signs and Wonders: Why Pentecostalism Is the World's Fastest Growing Faith*. Only a little more than 100 years old, it has over 100,000,000 adherents.

Numerically speaking, some of the most successful evangelists preach the Pentecostal gospel, including healing, tongues, slaying in the Spirit, holy laughter, and especially prosperity. The largest church in the world is a Pentecostal church in South Korea, the Yoido Full Gospel Church. At one time it claimed around 800,000 members; more recently the numbers are less (just 480,000 members in 2015, according to Wikipedia).

The German evangelist Reinhold Bonnke, whose message is Pentecostal to the core and who has worked mostly in Africa, makes spectacular claims. E.g., he says that in 2013 alone over one million of his hearers signed decision cards. One crusade (in the Ivory Coast) produced 456,589 such cards. One session of this crusade had an attendance of 250,000. Bonnke claims that he has conducted city-wide meetings in Africa "with as many as 1,600,000 people attending a single meeting using towering sound systems that can be heard for miles." Between 1978 and 2014, he says, about 73,000,000 people recorded personal decisions for Christ. Is this not evidence that God is working? Bonnke has said on his website that at an evangelistic meeting in Lesotho (Africa), he "told the people about the wonderful things God has been doing over the past 40 years" through his ministry. After a special meeting with African church leaders Bonnke said this "is only the beginning of what God will do in this beautiful nation and continue to do on this continent."

According to another web article, the *U.S. News and World Report* has said that "Mormonism is the fastest growing faith group in American history." Worldwide, in a recent year 60,000 Mormon missionaries produced 306,000 converts in 100 countries. From an even broader perspective, a Wikipedia article says that "Buddhism is being recognized as the fastest growing religion in western societies."

Wow! It would appear that God is at work all around us, in many different ways! Via Yahoo I did a web search of "what God is doing"; the first page said there were 325,000,000 results. One website is actually called *www.whatgodisdoing.com.* Another website says, "There is something infinitely significant about the time in which we live, so we'd best keep tuned to the big picture of what God is doing," especially regarding "global trends in the harvest force and the harvest fields" (i.e., missions).

This brings us back to our original question: what indeed IS God doing in the world? So far I have described several scenarios that raise this question, and which many would assume are clear-cut examples of how God is working among us. Now I will attempt to answer the question Biblically.

There are really three questions here. First, is God working in the world at all? If you are an atheist or a materialist or even a deist, you will obviously say NO. But the Christian says, YES, God is indeed at work in this world. Good apologetics can establish this rather quickly, applying especially the principle of sufficient cause. I will not address it in this study. Second, *how* does God work in the world? I.e., in what WAYS is He at work? And third, *how can we tell* if something is a work of God or not? What is the criterion or sign that an event or movement is "from God"?

We now begin to address the second question named above: *How does God work in the world?* Here there are two main answers. One is usually called Calvinism. This is the belief that God is the actual and ultimate cause of *everything* that happens, or "whatsoever comes to pass." He may use intermediate or secondary causes, as a man may use a lever to help him move a rock; but these secondary causes have no truly causative power.

For a Calvinist, every event is the product of God's eternal decree and omnicausal sovereignty. All church growth, every revival, every so-called spiritual advancement is a working of God. It is simple deductive reasoning: Whatever happens is caused by God; church renewal is happening; therefore church renewal is a work of God.

The problem here is that Calvinists cannot really distinguish between things God is doing and things God is NOT doing, since nothing falls into the latter category. Thus Calvinists must not only say that all church renewal is a work of God, but also that all church closings, all spiritual decline, all persecution of Christians, the origin and flourishing of Mormonism, and the spread of religions such as Buddhism and Islam—

are also things that "God is doing in the world." Most of us recognize immediately that such an approach is absolutely unbiblical.

So what is the other main answer to the question of *how* God works? I will call it the *Biblical* answer, and will now explain it as I understand it. The basic issue here is, what *kind* of God *is* God? He is indeed absolutely sovereign over all things. But does God have to be the *cause* of all things in order to be sovereign? This is one of Calvinism's basic assumptions, and it is indeed just an assumption—a presupposition without any real foundation. And in fact it is not true. The sovereign God of the Bible does not have to cause all things; indeed, His sovereignty is greater than that! He is able to create worlds permeated with relatively independent powers capable of originating events and decisions and actions, and still maintain sovereign control over them.

This leads to the next basic issue, namely, what kind of *world*—the world we live in—did God choose to create? Is it a pre-programmed, robotic world, in which human beings have no truly free will and in which even every sin and every evil result happens by God's design and God's causation? No! We reject this Calvinistic approach. Rather, God has created a world in which He has placed two systems that work according to a relative independence, i.e., the ability to act and to produce events not caused by God but still under God's control. These two systems or forces are *natural law* and *free will*. And here is the deal: Most of the things that happen in the world, by God's plan, are caused by these two forces, not by God.

This is the kind of God who exists, and this is the kind of world He has made.

Against this backdrop, we may now ask, *how* does God work in this world? We can distinguish four kinds of divine activities. First, there is what we can call *general providence*. This is by far the most common relationship God has with the world. Basically, He Himself is not actually acting or working, but is overseeing and allowing His relatively-independent world to make its own history by using the abilities He has implanted within it. The laws of nature govern regular and predictable changes in the atomic, mineral, plant, and animal domains. And we free-will beings—men, women, and children—interact with God, with one another, and with the world around us to create new events and to develop our environment and to inaugurate new paths into the future.

Where is God in this relatively-independent universe? In His omniscience (including His foreknowledge) and omnipresence, He is observing and monitoring every detail, from the greatest to the smallest. Other than being the Creator of such a world, does He have any part in its ongoing history? How does He exercise His sovereignty, under this *general* providence?

Here is where we talk about God's *permissive* will. As a corollary of his constant, universal surveillance of the world God is actively *permitting* every human plan and about-to-happen event to proceed into actuality. Along with this is a second corollary, namely, God's readiness and ability to *intervene* into any world circumstance in order to *prevent* or *alter* its potential course. For example, see James 4:13-15.

By His sovereign choice this is the kind of world God decided to make, including creatures with genuine free will. Thus according to His permissive will He allows us to use our free will to make decisions and to create events that are even contrary to His stated precepts and desires for us. I.e., He allows us to sin and to rebel against Him and to develop false belief systems and evil lifestyles. (This is not a *moral* permission, but a *physical* permission.) All such things are included within God's general providence.

The other three ways that God works in the world involve His active and deliberate intervention into the "natural" course of things and the normal flow of history. One of these (the second way He "works," overall) is what we call *special providence*. This would be an act by which God causes something new to happen in the world without violating a law of nature and without violating human free will. E.g., He may tweak the flow of natural law in order to influence or change our plans (see Job 37:6-7);

sometimes it works (e.g., Luke 12:20), and sometimes it does not (e.g., Amos 4:6-11). This involves the bestowing of special blessings (Job 37:13), including answers to prayers.

Another way that God works by intervening into the natural course of things (and the third way He works overall) is by what we call *miracles*. Miracles are more intense and dramatic than special providence because they are Acts of God which deliberately and visibly violate the laws of nature, mainly so that these Acts may function as evidence of the divine origin of an accompanying revelation. God does not work miraculously at random; He does so in connection with *new revelation*, which is given to explain *new redemptive works*. Thus we would expect miracles in the apostolic era, but not today.

The fourth and last kind of divine activity is what I call *supernatural spiritual events*. Here also God is definitely intervening into the natural flow of history, but this time on an invisible, spiritual level. This is unlike much special providence and most if not all miracles, in which God is interacting with the physical world in a visible way. Examples of supernatural spiritual events would be the Holy Spirit's work of inspiring prophets and apostles to speak God's revealed word, the incarnate presence of the eternal Logos in the man Jesus Christ, the propitiatory result of Christ's death, and the indwelling of the Holy Spirit and His saving activity within us.

These last three kinds of divine working in the world are the expression of God's *purposive* will, as distinct from His permissive will (which applies to general providence). In these three kinds of works (special providence, miracles, and supernatural spiritual events) God is acting within and upon the world to fulfill a specific purpose of some kind.

The information I have just been presenting has been in answer to the question of HOW God works in the world. The first and most common way God works is via the mostly passive general providence, in which God permits natural law and free will to cause things to happen. This applies to church activities as well as to everything else. The other three ways in which God works are deliberate interventions into the world in order to accomplish specific purposes by directly causing things to happen. Compared to the amount of things that happen in the world (including in the church) via general providence, the number of things that happen as special providence, miracles, and supernatural spiritual events are minuscule. They are significant and necessary, but relatively few.

Now we come to the question of how all of this applies to our main point of discussion, namely, exactly *what* is God doing in the world today, and *how can we tell* if something is a work of God or not? This is especially important, since most things that are happening are NOT active works of God but are the result of natural law and free will choices (i.e., general providence). Thus we ask, what is the criterion or sign that something is from God?

The things that happen under general providence are actually *caused* by ordinary natural law and ordinary human free-will choices and acts. These forces are almost constantly producing events that fall under God's *permissive* will. Thus the odds are that most things that happen both in our lives and in the church are combinations of these two forces. This is near the other end of the spectrum from Calvinism, which generally says that God is the cause of "whatsoever comes to pass," i.e., everything.

This does not mean that God is indifferent toward what we do with our free will, though. In fact, in His revealed Word He has given us directions and instructions about what He wants and requires us to do, and thus what we are obligated to do. We call this God's *preceptive* will (as distinct from His purposive and permissive wills). God's preceptive will falls into two general categories: His will about our *morality*, and His will about our *spirituality*. God's revealed will gives us a normative pattern for both.

I am using the word *morality* to refer to our general ethical behavior, or to the right and wrong actions especially regarding our relationships with other human beings. God's moral law says, e.g., "Do not steal. Do not murder. Do not lie. Do not commit sexual immorality."

What I am calling *spirituality*, on the other hand, is what some might think of as "religious" behavior, or things we do in connection with our direct relationship with God. This includes right knowledge and right worship of God, the right means of salvation from sin, and the right way to conduct ourselves as the corporate body of God's "chosen ones." All of this applies to God's will for the church, and for the way we participate in the church.

God's revealed preceptive will is one of the main things we are looking for when we study the Bible. Our first task is to make every effort to understand this will correctly. Despite our good intentions we do not always succeed in this effort. This is especially true in reference to spirituality (e.g., how to be saved, how to "be the church"). Our second task is to put our understanding of this preceptive will into practice, i.e., to obey God's will for morality and spirituality. Here is where our free will is used and is put to the test. Even regarding those things we understand aright, sometimes we choose to do the opposite. And God in His general providence and within His permissive will allows us to do wrong things, things that are contrary to His preceptive will.

Sometimes a wrong understanding of God's will and/or a perverse use of our free will leads to obviously disastrous results for individuals and for religious movements (e.g., the Jim Jones suicide cult in Jonestown, Guyana, in 1978). But sometimes, under God's general providence and permissive will, human understanding and/or choice leads to results that give an appearance of success, suggesting to many that God's hand of blessing must be at work therein, when it is actually not. This is especially true if there is a particularly forceful and inspirational human leader behind the work (e.g., the Mormon religion, or the ministries of evangelists such as Joel Osteen and Reinhold Bonnke). Other than His general providence and permissive will, we cannot expect God to be doing any positive work in such religions and ministries that are contrary to His revealed will.

The bottom line here is that when we apply the test of God's preceptive will as found in His Word, we must conclude that most of the things people assume are "the working of God in the world" are no such thing. We simply cannot accept the idea that God is working in movements that are teaching false doctrine and are contradicting His revealed purpose for the church, no matter how glamorous they look.

We now turn to the ways that God does indeed actively work in the world, i.e., the three ways He intervenes in the normal course of events. When we look within our own lives, and within the boundaries of Christendom in general, do we have any reason to believe God is working via special providence, or through miracles, and/or by means of supernatural spiritual activity? Is God's hand at work in any of these ways today?

I will re-emphasize a basic principle here, which is a corollary of the fact that God has revealed His moral and spiritual will to us: God will intervene to bless, encourage, and promote our deeds and labors, regarding both morality and spirituality, *only if we are striving to follow His revealed preceptive will*. Regarding God's will for our moral life, we should not, e.g., expect God to intervene and bless a fraudulent business deal, a dishonest sale of a faulty item, or an illicit affair. Regarding God's will for the spiritual life of the church, we should not, e.g., expect God to intervene and bless any religious group, denomination, or congregation which is based on falsehood and/or which is teaching false doctrine. Despite rapid growth, megachurch attendance figures, or high numbers of baptisms, God is not working in these situations! Other fActs that could account for such apparent success are cultural appeal, leadership with charisma, or even demonic deception and demonic miracles.

This being said, I do definitely believe that God works in our lives and in His churches, missions, and parachurch organizations via (first of all) His special providence, especially to answer our prayers for their protection and progress. This was a major way God worked among the Israelites in Old Testament times, and surely He is working this way today. A New Testament example of this is the way God "opened and closed doors" for Paul and other kingdom workers (2 Corinthians 2:12; Colossians 4:3; Romans 1:13; 15:22).

One problem with this, however, is another principle I adhere to, namely, that only inspired prophets can interpret God's special providence. Only inspired prophets can tell for sure if God is at work or not in this way. Sometimes it is a pretty sure conclusion that He is so working, as when He seems to be so obviously answering prayers for missionaries, for example. But sometimes God may, via special providence, be doing something to accomplish a purpose that we do not recognize, or something that seems to be completely negative rather than a positive blessing (e.g., Amos 4:6-11; Haggai 1:1-11), until explained by a prophet.

We should never doubt that God does so intervene today, though. This is why we continue to pray for missionaries, for church leaders, for the lost, and for help in discerning the true meaning and application of the Word of God. (About the last one, see my book, *Power from on High: What the Bible Says About the Holy Spirit*, College Press 2007, pp. 87-92.)

The second way God *can* intervene in the world in a special way is via miracles. There is no question that He did so in Bible times, but is this still happening? It is a fact that real miracles have been occurring in many religious circles in modern times, especially within Pentecostalism and the Charismatic Movement, and in connection with many individual ministries. The presence of these miracles is taken to be proof that God is working in these groups and ministries, and that He is thus blessing and approving them. I take the opposite view, however. I believe that the presence of genuine miracles in the exploding Pentecostal Movement and miracle-based ministries such as that of Reinhold Bonnke are proof that they are NOT from God.

I say this because I am convinced that the Bible teaches that God ceased to work *miraculously* once the completed New Testament became available to the church (i.e., around the end of the first century). This view is called *cessationism*, meaning that the miraculous gifts of the Spirit have *ceased* (see 1 Corinthians 13:8). I have explained this position and shown its Biblical basis in my books, *The Holy Spirit: A Biblical Study* (College Press, 2006), especially chapters 3, 7-10; and *Power from on High* (mentioned above), chapters 5, 8, 10-11.

Those who think miracles are a sure sign of God's work and God's approval today misunderstand not only God's purpose for His miracles, but also the reality and effect of demonic miracles. Satan and his demons have supernatural powers and are able to empower deceived human beings with the ability to work miracles (2 Thessalonians 2:8-12). If God is not working miracles today, and if Satan does work miracles in order to deceive the unwary, it is reasonable to conclude that the miracles that are happening today, even within broadly Christian contexts, are Satanic.

Those who doubt this and/or who emotionally reject it should look more closely at Matthew 7:21-23. Here Jesus describes one kind of Judgment Day scene. He speaks of people who try to make a case for being admitted into heaven based on the fact that they have done miraculous things during their lifetimes on earth. "Many will say to Me on that day, 'Lord, Lord, did we not prophesy in Your name, and in Your name cast out demons, and in Your name perform many miracles?'" It is significant that they are not just claiming to have done supernatural things, but are also pictured as doing them "in Your name"—speaking to Jesus. I.e., these are miracles performed in the context of Christendom, in the name of Jesus. But Jesus says to these miracle-workers, "I never knew you; depart from Me."

If this miraculous power is not coming from Jesus, then where is it coming from? The only reasonable conclusion is that it must be from Satan and his demons. But would Satan do these things in the very camp of the enemy? Think about it: what better way to wear his mask as an "angel of light" (2 Corinthians 11:14)? This is a major part of his overall work of deception. God will not do works in the context of false doctrine, but the devil is happy to do so.

The last way God intervenes into our world and works in our lives and in the church is through supernatural spiritual activities. For our purposes we will call attention to two main kinds of works of this nature, both of which are New Covenant activities of the Holy Spirit. One has to do with morality, the other with spirituality. The first relates to our efforts to obey God's preceptive will concerning morality or holiness; the other relates to our efforts to build up the church and make the church as effective as possible.

Regarding the former, God the Holy Spirit came into every Christian's personal world in Christian baptism (Acts 2:38-39). This is the time and place (Colossians 2:12) in which we received the gift of the indwelling presence of the Spirit to empower us to obey God's preceptive will for holiness (i.e., moral living). He is present within us at this very moment, ready to strengthen us with power (Ephesians 3:16) to resist temptation, to slay sin (Romans 8:13), and to be holy as God is holy (1 Peter 1:15-16). The more we allow God the Holy Spirit to work within us in this way, the more powerful the work of the church will be.

But there is more. God the Spirit works in our personal lives for *personal* growth in holiness, but he also works within us to empower us for leadership tasks in the church in order to produce *church* growth. This is what we think of as "spiritual gifts" or "gifts of the Spirit." When we think of "how God works in the world" or in the church today, this is one of the first things that should come to mind. God bestows tasks and abilities upon us, enabling us to lead, to speak, to teach, to encourage, to evangelize, to show mercy, etc., for the very purpose of building up the church as a whole. In this way God works in His people, through His people, and for His people.

If we look at this in the light of Ephesians 4:11-16, we see that one of the main purposes of this equipping work of God within the church is to build up the body of Christ "until we all attain to the *unity* of the faith, and of the knowledge of the Son of God" (vv. 12-13), and to a *maturity* in our understanding of sound doctrine and truth (vv. 13-15).

In this light, the real test of when God is working in the world, and especially in the church, is not really measured in terms of quantity—*how many* members, how many in attendance, how many converts, how many missional projects—but is measured in terms of faithfulness and commitment to truth and sound doctrine. Are we looking for examples of "what God is doing in the world"? Do we see our church developing unity and maturity of doctrine? We should be more thankful for and excited about a congregation of 100 that teaches truth and practices the true plan of salvation than a megachurch of 10,000 that teaches falsehood and gives sinners false hope.

As I noted in the beginning above, my teachers at Princeton said, "Find out where God is at work in the world, and join Him there." It really does not work that way. God has already told us what to do; He has revealed His preceptive will to us in His Word. He expects us to understand it and to put it into practice. He will help us do this, via the Spirit's indwelling and the Spirit's equipping gifts. Then, when we have faithfully undertaken to fulfill God's will for our lives and His church, *He will join us*, and work through us and with us. As Paul said, the Lord gives us the opportunity to serve (1 Corinthians 3:5). Then he said, "I planted, Apollos watered, but God was causing the growth" (1 Corinthians 3:6).

DID GOD RIG THE ELECTION?

QUESTION: What do you say to those who read Daniel 2:21 and say we did not have a choice in the [presidential] election? [Daniel 2:21 says that God "changes times and seasons; he removes kings and sets up kings."] Does this mean that God will raise up whomever he wants, and that now he has spoken and has decided to choose Donald Trump? This sounds almost as if God has rigged the election.

ANSWER: Let's begin by asking a more general question: Why does *anything* happen the way it does? What are the possible causes of any event that occurs? Actually there are only three possible causes for anything, namely, (1) God, (2) natural law, and (3) the decisions of free-will creatures. Regarding the outcome of the election, we can eliminate natural law. This leaves us with either God or human decisions.

Many people do indeed think that GOD caused Trump to be elected (or at least they wonder if this might be so). Before the election I saw this sentiment expressed often: "It really does not matter for whom you vote. God will decide who wins and who loses." A week or so after the election, one Facebook entry opined: "I believe that God has a reason why Trump won and I see why." (The writer did not see fit to share this reason with us, however.) And then we have the speculation above, that it seems "as if God has rigged the election."

This conclusion is based on a fairly common view of God, especially in view of Scriptures such as the one cited above. The view of which I speak is *theistic determinism*, known in its popular form as Calvinism. This is the idea that God is the ultimate and only real CAUSE of everything that happens. Natural law and human beings are intermediate or secondary causes: God works His will through them as instruments. In the final analysis, though, everything that happens is caused by God.

All true Calvinists believe this; many others have naively latched on to this idea and simply assume that this is what God must be like. True Calvinists, though, cite Biblical texts such as Daniel 2:21 (above) to prove their view. To this are added other texts, such as 1 Samuel 2:7, "The LORD makes poor and makes rich; he brings low and he exalts"; Job 34:24, "He shatters the mighty without investigation and sets others in their place"; Psalms 75:7, "It is God who executes judgment, putting down one and lifting up another"; and Daniel 5:21, "The Most High God rules the kingdom of mankind and sets over it whom he will" (ESV).

Thus it is a legitimate question: did God "rig" (i.e., determine) the result of the Trump-Clinton election, or any other modern election, for that matter? If not, then how can we understand these Biblical texts? The answer to the first question is NO; and to the second question the answer is that these texts must be understood in the historical context in which they were written, i.e., in the Old Covenant era. And this must be understood in the larger context of God's overall purpose for mankind, which is to surround himself with creatures made in His own image, whom He can love and who will freely choose to love Him in return.

The first and primary means by which God set out to accomplish this purpose was through the CREATION of the world (Genesis 1 and 2). But when His human creatures sinned and rebelled against Him (as He foreknew they would), God was ready to put into motion the supplementary means of accomplishing this purpose, namely, SALVATION. This was something that could be worked out only through the redemptive work of the God-man, Jesus Christ. But this task of saving human beings through Jesus Christ could be accomplished only after a lengthy period of PREPARATION for bringing the Savior into the world.

The point is this: most of the Bible (from Genesis 12 to the end of the Old Testament) is focused on this specific task of *preparing* for the first coming of Jesus. To work out His purpose, God chose Abraham's descendants through Isaac and Jacob—the nation of Israel—as his special physical family, and He worked with them specifically for about 2,000 years until the time was right for bringing Christ into the world. Thus almost the entire Old Testament is describing how God was working within the context of physical Israel, showing what He had to do to work out the preparation phase of His purpose.

This is the context in which the Scriptures cited above (Daniel 2:21, et al.) must be understood. They are talking about how God works to carry out His *purposive* will. These are the kinds of things God *could* do and actually *did* do in order to prepare for the incarnation of God the Logos as Jesus of Nazareth. If it is necessary for God to raise up the Pharaoh of the Exodus for a specific role in this purpose, then He causes it (Romans 9:17). If it is necessary to raise up or dethrone a particular king in order to accomplish His purpose, then God does it. If it is necessary for God to raise up Nebuchadnezzar and overthrow him, then He causes it (Daniel 5:18-21). See the same for Belshazzar (Daniel 5:22ff.). If it is necessary to raise up Cyrus for a certain role in this process, then God makes sure it happens (Isaiah 44:24-45:7).

But hear this: there is no reason to assume that God chooses and appoints every single governmental leader on every level in every tribe and nation in the whole world in every age! These texts tell us what God CAN do, and what he HAS done within the context of His purpose through Israel! But it is wrong to *generalize* or *universalize* these statements, as if they apply to everything that was happening (for example) in the Australian and North American continents in the Old Covenant era. Also, it is wrong to assume that they apply in the New Covenant era in the same way as in the Old, as if God were working through some physical nations today the way He worked through physical Israel in OT times. There is simply no basis for thinking that these texts apply to the American election in 2016 the same way they applied to Israel and her neighbors in OT times. Jesus specifically says (John 18:36) that His kingdom *is not of this world*. God is not working through any nation today—including the U.S.A. and modern Israel—as he worked during the period of preparation.

The bottom line is this: we have no reason to believe that God has any specific purpose for the U.S.A. as such, and no purpose for determining who was going to win the 2016 election in particular. Rather than assuming that everything has a purpose (as in Calvinism), we should assume that nothing has a purpose except those things God declares to be the case. And we can know this for sure only through the inspired words of a prophet of God: "For the Lord God does nothing without revealing his secret to his servants the prophets" (Amos 3:7).

I am not saying that God had no interest in and no part at all in the 2016 American election. Many people (including yours truly) prayed that God would intervene and bring about the result that will be best for his *spiritual* "nation" today, i.e., the church. I believe that God did so intervene through His special providence, to influence the outcome of the election. But sometimes God's providential intervention is ignored by his free-will creatures (Amos 4:6-11). Thus we cannot be sure whether the result of this or any other election is the result of God's purposive will, or instead whether it is the result of His permissive will. The Scriptures cited above cannot decide this.

In summary, we have no reason to think that Trump's victory was God's *purposive* will: God did not cause ("rig") it. It is much more likely (in my opinion) that it was the result of the choices made by free-will creatures under the *permissive* will of God, with some being influenced by God's *prescriptive* will (Romans 13:1-5; 1 Timothy 2:1-4) and by special (but resistible) providential intervention by God.

DOES GOD CARE HOW WE VOTE?

This is based on a sermon I preached at the First Church of Christ in Greendale, IN, on May 22, 2016.

I want to be clear about this from the beginning: I am not asking, "Does God *tell* us *for whom* to vote?" If this were my question, the answer would be simple: NO! I will not be naming names here, or endorsing anyone for office. My question, though, is very different from this: Does God *care* for whom we vote, or *how* we vote? And I do not mean simply in a presidential election; I mean, in *any* election? My answer to this question is YES.

Once we understand this, we will see that this question is indeed very relevant to the other question. Once we understand *why* God cares how we vote, it will be a lot easier to decide *for whom* to vote. Here I will explain why this is so. But first —

I.   IS THIS A LEGITIMATE QUESTION TO DISCUSS IN CHURCH?

Many Christians, as well as many non-Christians, will immediately challenge the legitimacy of discussing such an issue from the pulpit of a church. Many believe that the principle of "separation of church and state" should be invoked here. Sometimes that principle is expressed in a more down-home way, "Don't mix religion and politics!" In the pulpit you should just talk about Jesus! Just preach the gospel!

Well, I have news for you. Do you know who was the first person to "mix" politics and religion? You guessed it: GOD! *God Himself* mixes politics and religion when He tells us in the Bible what He wants and expects governments to do. What many people do not understand is that the Bible and Christianity are not just about "religion," or sin and salvation. The Bible is actually a *world view*: it is about *everything*! Its teaching is related to everything: education, economics, entertainment, work, family life, and—yes—politics! Or to put it in a more specific way— government.

Human government is God's idea and God's creation, and therefore has a purpose established by God. This divine origin is expressed in Romans 13:1-2, "Let every person be subject to the governing authorities. For there is no authority except from God, and those that exist have been instituted by God. Therefore whoever resists the authorities resists what God has appointed, and those who resist will incur judgment."

When Paul says, "There is no authority except from God," and "those that exist," he is not talking about specific kings or presidents or judges; he is talking about the various *kinds* of human authority that God has instituted within His creation. God alone has authority in Himself, as the sovereign Creator-God, but He has instituted several kinds of human authority. In the church, it is the elders; in marriage, it is the husband; in the family, it is the parents. And in the human population in general, it is *human government*, i.e., law-MAKERS, such as congress and the senate; and law-ENFORCERS, such as police, judges, and courts of law. God has instituted these specific systems of authority, but—and this is important—this does not mean that He determines every specific government or that He determines every specific ruler.

The point Paul is making is this: *whatever* form of government (e.g., republic, democracy, monarchy) a segment of the population chooses, those who have the roles of authority are *God's servants*, ideally carrying out God's purpose and God's will for that role. Romans 13:4 says specifically that anyone in a role of governmental authority "is God's servant" (Greek, *diakonos*), and verse 6 says that "the authorities are ministers of God" (Greek, *leitourgos*). Now, since God Himself has instituted government, and designated governing authorities as his servants, He must have a *purpose* for government and for those in roles of governing authority. There must be a divine reason why government exists.

This is, of course, why it is appropriate to discuss questions like "Does God care how we vote?" in the context of the church! In countries like the United States, we have the privilege of helping to select who will fill many of the positions of law-making and law-enforcing. And we Christians, more so than anyone else, have the inside track on knowing exactly what God wants these authorities to do! Thus the privilege of voting is a stewardship that has fallen into our hands. We have the ability to know God's purpose for government, and we have the ability to apply that knowledge on election day by voting for the candidates that are most likely to live up to God's purpose for them.

Let's examine this idea a little further.

II. HOW DOES THIS RELATE TO ELECTIONS AND VOTING?

As noted above, in Romans 13 God does not say that there must be just one specific type of government, whether dictatorship, democracy, monarchy, or something else. His purpose for government can be satisfied by most such forms. But God does specify *what every government is supposed to do*, i.e., he reveals the purpose for which he has established it. Thus God's Word, the Bible, tells us what God expects of governments. Actually, I believe this requirement is part of what is written on human hearts by virtue of our being made in God's image (Romans 2:14-15; cf. 1:32). It is a matter of reason, common sense, and moral intuition. But we are not left with just that. This aspect of God's law is revealed in the Bible!

And who today are the stewards or guardians of the Bible? God's people, CHRISTIANS! If anyone should know the purpose of government, it is we Christians!

So, in a country like the U.S.A., where we get to vote for government leaders, who is in the best position to know how best to vote? *Those of us who believe and understand the Bible!* What a privilege! What a responsibility! By voting, we are helping to put God's word into practice!

So, does God care how we vote? YES! ABSOLUTELY! Not only does he *care* how we vote; he *wants* us to vote, as guided by his Word! He wants us to vote for the candidates who, in our best judgment, are most likely to use the power of government to accomplish the purposes God's Word says they are supposed to accomplish!

This does not mean that the best candidate will always be a Christian. The issue is this: what does my candidate believe about the *purpose of government*? Does his or her view match what God has revealed? Some Christian politicians have a totally wrong understanding of this. One danger is that they will confuse the purpose and role of *government* (earthly kingdoms) with that of the *church* (Christ's Kingdom). We must understand that voting for a governmental leader is not the same as voting for an elder or a new minister. Whether the political candidate is a Christian or not is important to consider, but it is not the deciding factor. Sometimes an unbeliever may have reasoned his or her way to the Biblical view of the purpose of government, without realizing that he has come to the view that God has ordained. This may be the one for whom we should vote.

III. WHAT DOES THE BIBLE SAY IS GOVERNMENT'S PURPOSE?

The key question, then, is this: what does the Bible say government's purpose is? We must not look to the Old Testament for the answer to this question. God's dealing with Israel and her neighboring countries had a unique purpose and does not provide an example for anyone else. Instead, we look to several key New Testament texts, namely, Romans 13:1-7; 1 Timothy 2:1-4; and 1 Peter 2:13-14. When we analyze these teachings, we can sum of the purpose of government with the "two P's" — government's job is to PROTECT and to PUNISH.

Government's primary purpose is to *protect the rights* of every citizen. What are these "rights"? Actually, our American *Declaration of Independence* sums this up quite well when it says they include "life, liberty, and the pursuit of happiness." Life is God's gift to everyone. We have the right to stay alive. This applies to every person, even the unborn. Liberty or freedom is also a gift of God. He made us with free will, so that we are responsible for the way we live. This does not mean we are *morally* free to do whatever we want, since (as we have already seen) Romans 13:1-2 says God has established various forms of authority to which we must be subject. But within these limits we do indeed have such things as the freedom of speech, the freedom to worship God in truth, the freedom to work and play, and the freedom to own property. We also have the right to "pursue happiness," which means to live in peace, free from fear and from threats of harm and injustice. (We should also consider the "bill of rights," or the first ten amendments to the U.S. Constitution.)

This is all good, but the authoritative description of the rights government is supposed to protect are found in the Bible, specifically in 1 Timothy 2:1-4, "First of all, then, I urge that supplications, prayers, intercessions, and thanksgivings be made for all people, for kings and all who are in high positions, that we may **lead a peaceful and quiet life, godly and dignified in every way**. This is good, and it is pleasing in the sight of God our Savior, who desires all people **to be saved and to come to the knowledge of the truth**." This text says we should pray for those in government ("all who are in high positions"), but for what purpose and result? The fact that we are told to pray for specific results shows us that this is what God expects governments to do.

Included here in our God-inspired "bill of rights" are two main things. The first is the right to *live in peace and safety*, to "lead a peaceful and quiet life, godly and dignified in every way" (v. 2). This includes freedom from such fears as these: (1) The fear of international threats to our liberties, i.e., attacks from foreign enemies. This is a Biblical reason for governments to form armies. (2) The fear of criminal activities such as murder, rape, and theft. This is why governments have police forces of various kinds. (3) The fear of thoughtless and selfish behaviors such as reckless driving, intrusive noises, and "disturbing the peace" in general. This is why we have so many laws and rules that can be summed up in the word "justice"—our *right* to live in peace.

The second main right that we note in 1 Timothy 2 is the right to *serve God according to His instructions*. This is what we can call the "freedom of religion." It is government's job to provide an environment where we can live Godly lives and worship Him without interference. We should note that verse 4 implies that the government must protect our right to evangelize (share the gospel) and our right to proclaim the truth. In commanding us to pray for our government, God expresses His desire for "all people to be saved and to come to the knowledge of the truth."

The sad thing is that sometimes the government itself is the very entity that violates these rights rather than protecting them. Government does the very opposite of God's purpose for it by protecting abortion, destroying the family, and suppressing all Christian references in governmental contexts (such as public schools). These are things the U.S. government is doing; other governments are even much worse.

The point is this: the government's God-ordained responsibility is to *protect* these rights, i.e., to make sure that no one (including itself) prevents us from being able to do these things.

Here are two things we need to keep straight about "rights." First, no human being has a "right" to do just "anything he/she wants to do." For example, here is a quote from someone named William Powell, author of *The Anarchist Handbook*: "If I really want to do something, I don't care if its legal, illegal, moral, immoral, or amoral. I want to do it, so I do it." (From *Christianity Today*, 5/7/71, p. 25.) NO! This is not the meaning of "rights." Just because I may *want* to do something or am *able* to do something does not mean I have a *moral right* to do it. Especially—and this is crucial—we do not have the right to do anything that violates someone else's rights. It is specifically government's job to *legislate against* such activity, and to *punish* those who do such things. (See below.) Also, we do not have the right to do anything God has forbidden. For example, there is no such thing as "gay rights." Government should not specifically protect what God has specifically forbidden.

Here is a second thing to keep straight about "rights." As we have seen, government's job is to PROTECT our rights to various things, e.g., work opportunities, educational opportunities, ownership of property, health care. But it is NOT government's job to **PROVIDE** us with everything to which we have a right. Everyone has a right to a college education, but it is not government's job to provide everyone with a free college education. "Justice" is not equal *ownership*, but equal *opportunity*.

I said above that government's purpose can be summed up in the "two P's"—to Protect and to Punish. Protecting and preserving justice (rights) is the primary purpose, but part of the process of accomplishing this is included in government's *secondary* purpose, which is the ***punishment*** of wrongdoers. This purpose is clearly set forth in two texts. The briefer one is 1 Peter 2:13-14, which says, "Be subject for the Lord's sake to every human institution, whether it be to the emperor as supreme, or to governors as sent by him to **punish** those who do evil and to praise those who do good." In this context "evil" is injustice toward other people, and an "evildoer" is simply someone who has violated the rights of others.

The slightly longer text is Romans 13:3-4, "For rulers are not a **terror** to good conduct, but to bad. Would you have no **fear** of the one who is in authority? Then do what is good, and you will receive his approval, for he is God's servant for your good. But if you do wrong, **be afraid**, for he does not bear the sword in vain. For he is the servant of God, an **avenger** who carries out God's **wrath** on the wrongdoer."

We can see from this text that the punishment of evildoers by government has two purposes. One is that such punishment, when rightly applied, is supposed to be a *deterrent* to others who are potential wrongdoers, causing them NOT to do some evil thing they might want to do or have been thinking about doing. The text specifically says that rulers in this way are "a terror" to bad conduct. The one who contemplates doing wrong should "be afraid" of what will happen to him if he does it.

There is much debate over just how effective such punishment is in deterring crime. Whatever our feelings about this may be, we should know that there is another reason for punishing evildoers, namely, government should punish them *because they deserve it.* It is a matter of retribution, vengeance, payback, "you do the crime, you do the time." Romans 13:4 is clear about this: the government is an AVENGER who brings WRATH on the wrongdoer. One who violates another's rights should be punished because he deserves it, whether that deters someone else or not. And we should note this: the vengeance and wrath that government bestows on a criminal is *God's own vengeance and wrath,* because the government is God's minister and servant. This is how Romans 12:19 is fulfilled, where God speaks to non-government individuals: "Never avenge yourselves, but leave it to the wrath of God, for it is written, 'Vengeance is mine, I will repay, says the Lord.'" How does God repay? In eternal hell, yes (Hebrews 10:30), but in the context of Romans 12 and 13 he repays on this earth by the sword of civil government.

In summary, these two purposes of government—to protect and to punish—can be called *justice*: preserving justice for the innocent, and applying retributive justice to the guilty. This can also be called "LAW AND ORDER."

CONCLUSION

Our opening question was this: Does God care how we vote? It should be clear that the answer is YES! His revealed Word has given us His own description of what any government is supposed to do with its power and authority. We Christians of all people should be the ones who understand this and who try to put it into practice in whatever way we can. We could do so directly by personally running for some governmental office, or by getting a job in some governmental agency. A relatively few of us will do this, however. But every one of us who is of voting age can be a factor here by identifying as best we can which candidate's views get closest to the Biblical teaching above, and is therefore most likely to protect our rights and punish evildoers. We ourselves are serving God when we help to install a conscientious "servant of God" in public office!

What a **privilege** it is for us to have a *voice* in choosing law-makers and law-enforcers who can fulfill God's purposes for government!

What a **responsibility** it is for us to examine both the Biblical teaching on government, and to analyze the candidates' views to see who comes closest to the Biblical ideal.

What a **tragedy** it is when none of the candidates come anywhere near this Biblical ideal! Pray for wisdom, both for ourselves who vote and for those who are selected by vote.

"A WORLD LIKE THIS"

QUESTION: How can we explain the "natural" disasters that plague this world, such as the tornadoes, hurricanes, and floods that have occurred recently? Why would an all-loving and all-powerful Creator make a world like this?

ANSWER: Whenever a tragedy (like Hurricane Irma, for example) occurs, these sorts of questions will naturally arise. If God is an all-loving and all-powerful Creator, how can things like this happen? Why would God make a world like this—one with tornadoes, earthquakes, volcanoes, droughts, floods, and hurricanes that cause massive property loss and many human deaths?

The answer to this question lies in the key phrase: "a world like this." The common assumption is that this world—the one that is our present home—is the one God made "in the beginning" (Genesis 1:1). This, however, is not the case. This world, this physical universe in which we now live, is *not the same world* that God originally created. Not only that— it is *not the same world* that will be our future, eternal home.

In the beginning God created a universe of beauty and harmony, a universe designed to support and maintain a race of mortal yet undying human beings. Our relationship with the world was one of peaceable accord and cooperation. There was a condition, however: the continuation of this ideal arrangement depended (by God's plan) on mankind's responsible use of their divinely-given free will.

We do not know all the details of this primary stage of the universe. We do not know how basic forces such as climate, winds, precipitation, and seasons were controlled. We know that none of these phenomena would have posed a threat to human existence, but we do not know how all of them operated in the beginning (compared with the way they operate now).

What we do know is that serious negative changes in the natural universe occurred when the first human beings (Eve and Adam) used their gift of free will to sin against the Creator (Genesis 3:1ff.). Genesis 3 itself describes three of these changes: pain in childbirth for women, making a living through toilsome effort, and physical human death.

The second of these indicates that the curse was not limited to the bodies of human beings, but extended to the physical universe as a whole: "Cursed is the ground because of you" (Genesis 3:17). It is as if the canker of sin and the tentacles of the divine curse penetrated and permeated the entire creation, altering and disrupting its original harmony. We do not know the details of this devastation, but Romans 8:19-22 (NASB) affirms it:

> For the anxious longing of the creation waits eagerly for the revealing of the sons of God. For the creation was subjected to futility, not willingly, but because of Him who subjected it, in hope that the creation itself will also be set free from its slavery to corruption into the freedom of the glory of the children of God. For we know that the whole creation groans and suffers the pains of childbirth together until now.

The result of the primal sin and its consequences is that the world we live in today is simply *not* the paradise-like universe God made for human beings in the beginning. It does not always cooperate with us, but in many ways fights against us. To be sure, the world still declares the glory of God (Psalms 19:1); it still provides wonderfully for our needs (Matthew 5:45; 6:33; 1 Timothy 6:17); and we are still able to "subdue it" (Genesis 1:28)—

up to a point. But sometimes, more often than we would like, the cosmic curse rears its ugly head in the form of tornadoes and hurricanes and tsunamis, and reminds us not only that we are mortal beings but also that we are a sinful race.

Where, then, is the goodness of God in all of this? We have already seen two forms of it: the original innocent and bountiful nature of the pre-sin universe, and the bounty and beauty of the present cosmos (Acts 14:17; James 1:17) that still filter down to us through the darkness and deformity of this fallen world.

But regarding this divine love and goodness, there is more—*much* more! Yes, the original glorious version of the universe no longer exists. Yes, the one we call "home" is full of suffering and futility and corruption. But the deal is this: there is yet to come a *third* version of this "visible universe" (Colossians 1:16), this "heavens and earth"—a perfect and incorruptible form of the physical cosmos that will be the eternal home of the redeemed family of God!

This is the glorious hope with which Paul is comforting us in Romans 8:18-23. He sums it up in verse 18: "For I consider that the sufferings of this present time are not worthy to be compared with the glory that is to be revealed to us." This is when the cosmos will be "set free from its slavery to corruption into the freedom of the glory of the children of God" (v. 21). Having experienced "the redemption of our body" (v. 23), and being clothed with an imperishable body of glory and power (1 Corinthians 15:42-43), we will be free to roam about and probe into "the new heavens and a new earth, in which righteousness dwells" (2 Peter 3:13; see Revelation 21:1ff.). This will be the Phoenix-like universe that will arise out of the ashes of the final holocaust that will bring this present universe to an end (2 Peter 3:10-12).

To be sure, in this present world there is much pain and grief, and plenty of tears and sorrows. The tornadoes and floods and droughts will still come. But in anticipation of that promised new age and that coming new world, we can cry out with Paul, "Death is swallowed up in victory. O death, where is your victory? O death, where is your sting? … but thanks be to God, who gives us the victory through our Lord Jesus Christ" (1 Corinthians 15:54-57).

"Therefore, my beloved brethren, be steadfast, immovable, always abounding in the work of the Lord, knowing that your toil is not in vain in the Lord" (1 Corinthians 15:58).

CHILDREN OF GOD
ROMANS 8:14-25

This is a sermon I preached at the First Church of Christ in Greendale, IN, on April 29, 2018—the day before my 80th birthday.

The subject here is "The Children of God"—but how many of us feel like children? It is often said, "You are only as old as you feel." My problem with that is this: I *feel* old! When a man gets to be 80 years old, he is surely an "old man"!

I guess I could think of it as finally becoming an adult. But that just reminds me that the transition from childhood to adulthood is not that simple. When I was young, one was not considered to be an adult until age twenty-one. Today in most countries the age of eighteen is the "age of majority," as it is called. I saw recently that in Washington D.C. the city council is considering allowing 16-year-olds to vote.

My advice would be this: don't be in such a hurry! Many of us older folks can tell you — becoming an adult is not easy. You get married, then become parents, then become parents of teen-agers who want to be adults. Then you become grandparents, and before long you may become parents to your parents. It all makes us want to say, "O, to be young again!" I googled that phrase, and it said there were 31,300,000 entries. At the beginning (which is as far as I got) there were many poems, such as the following by Rex Rogers:

"Oh, to be young again,

    To run barefoot through the woods, hollows, and glens,

To see Grandpa, the old farm,

    And my dog Peppie running in the wind ... .

Well, go ahead and get nostalgic, because I am going to help you think of yourself as being "young again"! This sermon is on the subject, "CHILDREN OF GOD." For those of us who are Christians, this is who we are: children of God! In our text we are called children, even those of us in our 80s and 90s. Let's begin with Romans 8:14-17 (ESV):

> [14] For all who are led by the Spirit of God are sons of God. [15] For you did not receive the spirit of slavery to fall back into fear, but you have received the Spirit of adoption as sons, by whom we cry, "Abba! Father!" [16] The Spirit himself bears witness with our spirit that we are children of God, [17] and if children, then heirs—heirs of God and fellow heirs with Christ, provided we suffer with him in order that we may also be glorified with him.

Please do not get upset that verses 14 and 15 refer only to "sons of God." The word "sons" is used to distinguish us from slaves. In 2 Corinthians 6:18 the language is quite inclusive: "'I will be a father to you, and you shall be sons and daughters to me,' says the Lord Almighty." And here in Romans 8:16 it is clearly stated: "We are children of God." (Here the Greek word is *teknon*, which refers to the dependent child in a parent-child relationship.)

As we age, we may sometimes forget that in our relationship with God, we are in many ways *still His children*. As a Christian, no matter how old you are, you are still a child — a child of God. And our text, Romans 8:14-25, tells us three things about our status as children of God.

I. WE ARE *ADOPTED* CHILDREN OF GOD.

The first thing we learn here is that, as part of God's family, we are *adopted* children. Verse 15 says, "You have received the Spirit of adoption as sons." This is similar to Ephesians 1:5, "In love he predestined us for adoption through Jesus Christ." The Greek word is *huiothesia*, which in Greek culture was a technical or legal term for adoption. It is based on the word for "son," *huios*, but it was used for both male and female children.

It is important to emphasize that being adopted does not mean we are second-class children having only a "pseudo-sonship" status in God's family. It is true that some have adopted children for selfish or even evil reasons. In early 2018 a woman named Paula Sinclair from Richmond, Texas, was sentenced to 35 years in prison for adopting seven special-needs toddlers and keeping them locked in a very small bedroom for over ten years. She fed them only two meals of rice and beans per day. When they were finally rescued they were filthy, malnourished, dehydrated, and covered with bed-bug bites. (The state of Texas, of course, pays adoptive parents of special-needs children several hundred dollars per month in subsidies per child.) This is an extreme case; nevertheless, many think that there is some sort of stigma that comes with being adopted.

That is definitely not the case with our status as God's adopted children! Remember that Ephesians 1:5 says He adopted us "in love"! We are his *real* children—signed, sealed, and delivered, with all the rights, honors, and privileges pertaining thereto! When I think of our adoption into God's family, I think of Shawnee and Rob Fleenor, former students and co-workers when I was teaching in Cincinnati. Several years ago Shawnee and Rob adopted three precious babies from the Far East (I'm not sure which country) who have some special needs, and these children are treated like royalty! I know that because I see happy pictures of them on Shawnee's Facebook posts every so often, and she always refers to them as her *treasures*! That's who we are to God! We are His *treasures*!

Why is it, then, that we are just *adopted* children of God? Why do we not have the status of natural-born children? There are two reasons for this. One is that there was a time when we were *not* children of God. Just being a human being does not count here; you have to be a Christian to belong to God's family. We all went through the adoption process when we obeyed the gospel by believing in Jesus, repenting of sins, confessing our faith in Christ, and being immersed into union with Him. That is how we *became* God's children. Here is one way this is described: "But to all who did receive him [i.e., Jesus], who believed in his name, he gave the **right** to **become** children of God, who were born, not of blood nor of the will of the flesh nor of the will of man, but of God" (John 1:12-13).

Another reason why our status is that of adoption is because that distinguishes us from the sonship of Jesus, who is the one-and-only truly natural Son of God. Jesus's physical birth and the sonship that came from it were unique (see Luke 1:35). Jesus is described as God's *monogenēs* son (John 3:16). Most of us know the translation, "His only-begotten Son." The word means "unique, one-of-a-kind, one-and-only"; some Bible translations use those words in John 3:16. As God's children we do have some things in common with Jesus, as we shall see below; but it is important to remember that Jesus and His sonship are in a class by themselves.

Okay, we are *adopted* children of God. What else does our text say about our privileges of having God as our Father?

II. GOD IS OUR *ABBA* FATHER.

The second thing about our status as children of God is the very *close relationship* we have with Him. Our text, in verse 15, says that when we "received the Spirit of adoption as sons" (referring to the indwelling Holy Spirit), the Spirit enables us to cry out to God or address God as "Abba! Father!" Galatians 4:5 refers to our adoption as sons of God, then says in verse 6, "And because you are sons, God has sent the Spirit of his son into our hearts, crying, 'Abba! Father!'"

"Abba" is a word from the Aramaic language, which is similar to Hebrew and which was spoken by most Jews (including Jesus) in the New

Testament era. It is a term of endearment or intimacy, used by a child who truly loves and feels close to his or her father. It is similar to the way we address our fathers as "Daddy" or "Papa." The gospels report one occasion where Jesus used this intimate name for His Father in heaven. This was in the Garden of Gethsemane, as He was agonizing over the prospect of his atoning death for our sins: "Abba, Father, all things are possible for you. Remove this cup from me. Yet not what I will, but what you will" (Mark 14:36). I can think of Jesus here folding Himself into the arms of and upon the lap of His heavenly Father.

It sounds quite natural for Jesus to call the Father "Abba." But for the rest of us to do so, it sounds in some ways like a contradiction! How dare we call the infinite, sovereign Creator and Lord of the universe—"Daddy"? God is majestic and holy; we are puny and sinful creatures! How can we do such a thing? Yet—God makes it plain here in this text; He says we can call Him "Abba! Daddy!" This shows us that even though He is indeed the transcendent Creator, *He loves us as His own dear children!* As 1 John 3:1 says, "See what kind of love the Father has given to us, that we should be called children of God—and so we are."

As God's children we must learn to balance these two attitudes. On the one hand, we must worship God in "fear and trembling." As Philippians 2:12 says, you must "work out your own salvation with fear and trembling." This is not talking about how we receive forgiveness of sins, but how we must always be concentrating on the sanctification aspect of our salvation—trying to live better and better in order to please our heavenly Father. Also, the "fear" is not the idea of "being afraid" of God, with the fear of terror. This is the word *phobos*, which also in some contexts (as here) means the fear of reverence, respect, and awe before God. See how the NIV translates 2 Corinthians 7:1, that we should be "perfecting holiness out of reverence [*phobos*] for God."

But on the other hand, as is shown here in Romans 8:15, we must also be able to reach out and clasp the hand of God and call him "Daddy"! Some do not see both sides of this balanced relationship. I had a professor in Bible college who would not let us speak to God in prayer as "Dear Father" or "Dear God." He considered using the word "dear" as too familiar and too intimate! But this is what God wants! Because He loves us, He wants us to love Him: "We love because he first loved us" (1 John 4:19). Though the Greek does not have the pronoun "him," many translations add it here because that seems to be the meaning in the context: "We love HIM, because He first loved us!"

When we can reach this "Abba" level of love for God, this means that we have a comforting assurance of our relationship with Him. As the Apostle John says in 1 John 4:16, "We have come to know and to believe the love that God has for us." In verse 17 he adds, "By this is love perfected with us, so that we may have confidence for the day of judgment."

What a blessing it is to be able to call God our "Abba"—and to know that He Himself is the One who has made this relationship possible by adopting us as His dear children!

III. WE ARE GOD'S *HEIRS*.

There is one more implication from the fact that we are God's children, and that is stated in Romans 8:17. Yes, we are God's children, "and if children, then heirs—heirs of God and fellow heirs with Christ"! We will inherit God's fortune!

Inheritance is the usual result of a parent-child relationship. Someday we will receive our parents' possessions, even if we are adopted children. Sometimes this whole inheritance system can be the source of enmity and resentment and division within a family. However, the Bible itself teaches that leaving an inheritance for one's children is expected in a family relationship and is part of what it means to be loving parents. "For children are not obligated to save up for their parents, but parents for their children" (2 Corinthians 12:14). To carry it a generation further, "A good man leaves an inheritance to his children's children" (Proverbs 13:22)!

So, with God as our Father, and our status as His children, we have an inheritance coming! When I think of this, my mind wanders to something that happens frequently on the daily TV show "Wheel of Fortune." Every day there is a prize puzzle on the wheel, which is always a rather desirable trip to a fancy resort area such as the Bahamas or Oahu. When the person who wins that round thus wins that trip, he or she often jumps up and down and cries out, "Where am I going? Where am I going?" Sometimes we are quite slow in coming to realize just how great our salvation is, but when the fact that we are God's heirs finally sinks in, how can we help but jump up and down, and yell, "Where am I going? Where am I going?"

Then the answer comes to us from God's Word, loud and clear, "GLORY!" As God's heirs we get to go to GLORY! See Romans 8:17-18, "And if children, then heirs—heirs of God and fellow heirs with Christ, provided we suffer with him in order that we may also be **glorified** with him. For I consider that the sufferings of this present time are not worth comparing with the **glory** that is to be revealed to us." We note here that we are not only heirs of God, but also *fellow heirs* with Christ, the one-and-only natural Son of God! Think about it: *we get what He gets!* And what does Jesus inherit? What does He get? He gets GLORY! A glorious new resurrection body, and all the glories of heaven itself! And the Bible says here that *we* are "glorified with Him," with a glory that will one day be revealed to us! What is included in this one word, glory, as it describes our inheritance? Two things are emphasized in our text: a *new universe*, and a *new body*. See Romans 8:18-23,

> [18] For I consider that the sufferings of this present time are not worth comparing with the glory that is to be revealed to us. [19] For the creation waits with eager longing for the revealing of the sons of God. [20] For the creation was subjected to futility, not willingly, but because of him who subjected it, in hope [21] that the creation itself will be set free from its bondage to corruption and obtain the freedom of the glory of the children of God. [22] For we know that the whole creation has been groaning together in the pains of childbirth until now. [23] And not only the creation, but we ourselves, who have the first fruits

of the Spirit, groan inwardly as we wait eagerly for adoption as sons, the redemption of our bodies.

In this text the universe around us is personified as itself waiting eagerly for the time when our inheritance becomes available, because this present universe has been corrupted by sin and longs to be set free from things like addictions and disease and death that cause us so much suffering. So it "waits with eager longing" (v. 18) for the day when the final fruits of our sonship will be passed along to us. This will include a new or renewed universe that has been "set free from its bondage to corruption" (v. 21). This will be the "new heavens and a new earth in which righteousness dwells" (2 Peter 3:13), and following the Judgment Day this will be the Father's inheritance gift to the whole family of His children (see Revelation 21 and 22). This is what Jesus meant when He said, "The meek shall inherit the earth" (Matthew 5:5).

But that's not all. Yes, we will live forever and ever in this glorified universe, but what about our own selves? What about these uncomfortable, aging, aching bodies? Well, the other part of our inheritance is that we will get a new body for living in the new universe! That will be the zenith of our inheritance, the crowning glory compared to the whole universe of glory in which we will live. As Romans 8:23 says, this is what we are groaning inwardly and waiting eagerly for: "the redemption of our bodies." A new body! A redeemed body! A glorified body!

Before going further, let me ask a question: What do we have *more and more* of, the older we get? Many answers could be suggested, but I will focus on two. This is the one that most old people think of first: PAIN! (Or suffering.) And this is what makes our expected inheritance of a new body all the more special! See how Paul describes it in Romans 8:18: "For I consider that the sufferings of this present time are not worth comparing with the glory that is to be revealed to us"! Our present sufferings are the result of the curse upon our bodies and upon the physical universe described in Genesis 3, a curse that ends in physical death.

Remember a song we sang in church as children? "Head and shoulders, knees and toes, knees and toes, knees and toes! Head and shoulders knees and toes—all belong to Jesus!" Well, you can still sing that as you reach old age; but as you get older, it takes on a whole new meaning: "Head and shoulders, knees and toes—all feel painful!"

This is why being children of God is so wonderful! Yes, we go through sufferings here, and it's sad and difficult. But these sufferings "are not worth comparing with the glory" that lies ahead! Paul said the same thing in 2 Corinthians 4:17, "For this slight momentary affliction is preparing for us an eternal weight of glory beyond all comparison"! What is this "eternal weight of glory"? It includes *a new body*, just like the one Jesus has now! A body of glory! See Philippians 3:21, which says that Jesus "will transform our lowly body to be like his **glorious** body"!

I said above that as you get older, there are two things that you get more and more of. One is pain. What is the other? If you are a Christian— if you are a child of God—the second thing that increases day by day as you get closer and closer to the end of this present life is this: HOPE! The *hope* of receiving our inheritance grows and grows, and looms larger and more precious moment by moment! Here is what Paul says about it (Romans 8:24-25): "For in this hope we were saved. Now hope that is seen is not hope. For who hopes for what he sees? But if we hope for what we do not see, we wait for it with patience."

Biblical hope is not just the fanciful longing that we mean when we say things like "I *hope* I win the Publishers' Clearing House sweepstakes!" Seven thousand dollars a week for the rest of your life would be nice, but we don't really expect it, given the astronomical odds! But Biblical hope is much different. It is actually the feeling of *assurance*. Biblical hope is a confident expectation of something good that is still in the future. Our text emphasizes the element of futurity: we don't have it yet. And certainly, the object of our hope is something good. No, actually, as Tony the Tiger says, "It's GREAT!" Its greatness is summed up in the word GLORY. "Christ in you, the hope of glory" (Colossians 1:27)!

But the main point I want to stress is that Biblical hope is an attitude of the heart, the attitude of *confident expectation*. It is another word for the *assurance of salvation*. And if you are a child of God, this should be getting stronger and stronger as you get closer to the end of this present life of suffering. We should be saying with Paul, "To live is Christ, to die is gain … . My desire is to depart and to be with Christ, for that is far better" (Philippians 1:21, 23).

Because we have this hope, i.e., this assurance, we have a specific attitude toward our coming death and our future glory. As Romans 8:25 says, we wait eagerly for it with patience—or perseverance, as some versions translate it. Patience? Perseverance? I like to express it as *patient endurance*. The point is — *don't give up* while you are waiting for the glory that is the object of your hope!

Paul also says in verse 25 that we are *waiting eagerly* for that glory. When the ESV translates it simply as "wait for it," that does not do justice to the word. It is the same word (*apekdechomai*) that is used in verse 23 and translated "wait eagerly." That is what it means in verse 25: we are waiting for our inheritance with a strong, happy expectation! The sufferings of this present time are nothing compared to that glory that awaits us! As I once wrote about "the weight of glory" in 2 Corinthians 4:17, "In terms of weight, the sufferings hardly show up on the scale at all, while the coming glory presses it all the way down." The more hope we have, the less fear we have of death and judgment. Let us always be aware of that wonderful inheritance that awaits us!

CONCLUSION

I read something recently in a Facebook post. It was a quote from Corrie ten Boom, whose ministry to persecuted Jews and to fellow prisoners in a Second World War prison camp is legendary. She gave this counsel: "Hold everything in your hands lightly, otherwise it hurts when God pries your fingers open." But there is more.

It is meaningful to me that the Facebook post that I was reading was written by my daughter, Susan Cottrell Meyer, who is a hospice nurse. She deals with people who are closing in on death every day. She had been rereading Corrie ten Boom's famous book, *The Hiding Place*. Here is what Susan said: "As a nurse, a line near the end touched me. [Corrie] was talking about … sharing the gospel in the concentration camp. 'Deathbeds became gateways to heaven.' When my job becomes drudgery, I try to remember that."

My message to you today is this: if you are a child of God, it is good to remember that at all times.

THE PARADOX OF PRAYER
JAMES 5:13-18

The paradox of prayer may be stated like this: If God can do whatever He chooses, and if He really loves us, why doesn't He answer all of our prayers? Here I will comment on James 5:13-18, and will use this text to help resolve the paradox of prayer. Here is the NASB version of this text:

> [13] Is anyone among you suffering? *Then* he must pray. Is anyone cheerful? He is to sing praises. [14] Is anyone among you sick? *Then* he must call for the elders of the church and they are to pray over him, anointing him with oil in the name of the Lord; [15] and the prayer offered in faith will restore the one who is sick, and the Lord will raise him up, and if he has committed sins, they will be forgiven him. [16] Therefore, confess your sins to one another, and pray for one another so that you may be healed. The effective prayer of a righteous man can accomplish much. [17] Elijah was a man with a nature like ours, and he prayed earnestly that it would not rain, and it did not rain on the earth for three years and six months. [18] Then he prayed again, and the sky poured rain and the earth produced its fruit.

I.   COMMENTS ON THE TEXT.

Verse 13 — "Suffering" means any time things are going bad for you in any way. "Cheerful" means any time things are looking good for you in any way. In either case, we should *talk to God* about it — either in petition or in praise.

Verse 14 — This is very important: the word "sick" can refer to *physical illness* or *spiritual weakness*. It is likely that James has both in mind. When elders are called, they first apply oil to the sick person, for medicinal purposes (Isaiah 1:6; Luke 10:34; Mark 6:13) and perhaps for a symbolic purpose, representing God's blessing. The *main* thing elders do in this situation is pray over the sick, for their healing.

Verse 15 — The word for "restore" (*sōzō*) is the usual word for "save." Sometimes it means "to heal a *physically* sick person." But—and this is very important—sometimes it refers to salvation from *sins* (see 5:20). There are two kinds of restoration: being "raised up" from the physical illness, and being forgiven of sins.

Verse 16 — As in v. 15, the word used here for "healed" can refer to physical healing, *or* to spiritual healing from sins (for the latter, see John 12:40; Acts 28:27; 1 Peter 2:24). Sometimes there is a connection between physical sickness and sinful deeds; thus confession of sins is necessary for physical healing.

Verses 17-18 — Elijah is an Old Testament hero who prayed some mighty prayers: that God would raise a dead boy to life (1 Kings 17:22), that God would send fire from heaven to consume an offering (1 Kings 18:36ff.), that God would stop and start rain in Israel (1 Kings 17, 18). Why is *Elijah* cited as an example for us? After all, he was a prophet and a miracle-worker, and we are not! Answer: because he was still *just a man*. He had no more inherent personal power than you or I. The answers to his prayers came from God.

II. APPLICATION TO OUR PRAYER LIFE

Having commented on the passage from James, I will now apply this text (and other Biblical teachings) to three kinds of prayer.

A. First are the prayers God will NEVER answer.

Here are two aspects of this kind of prayer. The first is prayers that are contrary to God's *nature*, contrary to *who God is*. For example, God is a rational, logical being. He will not answer a prayer to do something that contradicts logic, e.g., a prayer to make a square circle. For another example, it is God's nature to exist on a time line, with a past and a future. For God, the past is past and the future is future. Thus He will never answer prayers to change the past. Also, God is a *holy* being; He cannot do anything that is morally evil. Thus He will not answer prayers that make it easy for us to sin.

The second kind of prayer that God will never answer is prayers that are contrary to His *purposes*. What purposes are these? We may begin with His purpose of CREATION, which includes His purpose of creating beings with free will. When God created us with free will, it was His purpose to make our relationship with Him depend on our own free-will choices. Thus, God will *not* answer prayers that require Him to violate our free will. Specifically, He will never answer our prayers for the lost that require Him to *force* or *cause* a sinner to believe. See Matthew 23:37. Of course, God can and will do all sorts of things that *influence* a lost person toward faith, without pushing him over the line. So it is still valid to pray for the lost. But in the end, accepting Christ must be the lost person's own free choice.

Another main purpose of God is His purpose of REDEMPTION. He will never answer a prayer that interferes with His "predetermined plan" to save us from sin and restore us to fellowship with Himself (Acts 2:23)—even if that prayer is prayed by Jesus himself (Luke 22:42)!

A third purpose of God—one that we often do not think about—is His purpose of placing this physical world under a CURSE. Once sin entered the world, it was God's purpose to put a curse upon the entire physical creation (see Genesis 3, and Romans 8:18-22). This curse is summed up in the word *death*, but includes much more.

Christ's work of atonement and resurrection laid the groundwork for removing this curse on the physical world, but it will not actually be done until the Second Coming of Jesus, by means of the resurrection of our bodies and the making of the new heavens and new earth. Sickness and death are not natural for human beings, but they are a part of the world as we know it: *fallen* and *cursed*.

This is why God will not answer prayers that remove this curse ahead of time. (E.g., see Hebrews 9:27.) So there is no need to pray that we will *never* get sick, get old, or die. These physical evils are not a part of the original creation purpose, but they are a part of the curse placed on the creation as a result of sin. God may give *temporary* relief from the curse: He may heal sickness, ease pain, postpone death, protect from storms. Obviously He does this in answer to some prayers. But here is the point: these are *exceptions* to the general purpose of the curse, and we cannot complain if our prayers in this area are not answered. James 5 should be read in this light.

So, living in this fallen and becursed world is like living on a hillside, down which is flowing toward us a steady sea of volcanic lava. We can pray for God to enable us to endure it, or temporarily avoid it, but ultimately it will engulf us. This is part of the fruit of sin.

B. Next are prayers God MAY or MAY NOT answer, according to his choice.

Let us be assured that God has complete sovereignty over the laws of nature. He can "tweak" or manipulate them by means of His special providence (as with the weather, Job 37:12-13); He can even suspend or bypass them (as with miracles, e.g., the ten plagues on Egypt). Because the purpose of miracles is related to new revelation from God that is connected with new redemptive works of God, we do not expect God to work miracles in our everyday lives. But He can and He does indeed intervene in the world via His special providence.

Because God can and does sometimes "tweak" the laws of nature in answer to our prayers, this is why we should always pray in accordance with the instructions in James 5. God can even cause people to die, if He has reason to do so (see 2 Samuel 12). He can raise people from the dead, if He has a reason to perform such a miracle (e.g., Elijah and the widow's son; Jesus and Lazarus). He can also make sick people well (as King Hezekiah, Isaiah 38; and Epaphroditus, Philippians 2:27). Remember, sickness and death are the essence of the curse upon the world because of sin. This curse has been *reversed* by the death and resurrection of Jesus; nevertheless it will not be *removed* until His second coming.

But here is the point: in individual cases, God can and sometimes does intervene, and sometimes heals, or eases pain, or slows down a killer disease, or gives new insight to doctors, or gives inner peace. Thus we should *always* pray for God to thus intervene. This is one point that James 5:13-18 is making: the prayer of faith will restore the sick! Sometimes God will answer such prayers, giving temporary and exceptional relief from the curse; so we should never cease offering them up to Him.

But here is "the paradox of prayer" that continues to haunt us: even though God is all-powerful and truly loves us, sometimes he will decide NOT to answer such prayers. Why not? Because God always sees a *bigger picture* than we do, and He knows of an ultimate good that will result from allowing the present course to continue. In a sense it is the same reason why loving parents, even those with unlimited means, do not always grant every request of their children. As the old TV show title rightly said, "Father knows best!" And our heavenly Father knows best of all, since He is indeed all-knowing and all-wise. Thus, sometimes, in His infinite wisdom, God knows that a *better* purpose will be accomplished by *not* answering our prayers; so we must trust His wisdom.

For example, Elijah prayed for God to take his life (1 Kings 19:4), but God did not answer this prayer! Paul prayed for God to remove his "thorn in the flesh" (2 Corinthians 12:7-9), but God did not answer this prayer! As an old song by Garth Brooks says, "Sometimes I thank God for unanswered prayers." The bottom line is this: we must trust the wisdom of God, and trust His promise in Romans 8:28, "And we know that God causes all things to work together for good to those who love God, to those who are called according to *His* purpose." Thus when we pray, we must always say, "If the Lord wills" (James 4:15).

C. The third kind of prayer is prayers God will ALWAYS answer.

Someone might think that there is no kind of prayer that God will *always* answer, but there is such prayer. Specifically, God always answers a *sinner's* prayer for personal *salvation*. Remember, James is writing about not just physical sickness, but also about the spiritual sickness of sin. The prayers he is talking about are not just prayers for the healing of physical sickness—which God may or may not answer. But he is also talking about prayers for salvation from sin — which God will *always* answer when they come from a heart of sincere repentance and faith.

God has *always* been willing to answer this prayer: "Whoever calls on the name of the Lord will be saved." See Joel 2:32; Romans 10:13; Acts 22:16; 1 Peter 3:21. Ananias said to Saul of Tarsus: "Now why do you delay? Get up and be baptized, and wash away your sins, calling on His name" (Acts 22:16). This "calling on his name" in Christian baptism is the only true and Biblical "sinner's prayer."

If you are not a Christian, you can pray this prayer *right now*, and you can see it answered with your own eyes, when you meet Jesus in Christian baptism! 1 Peter 3:21 says that *baptism now saves you*, not by washing dirt off your body, but because it is an *appeal to God* — a prayer to God, a calling upon the name of God — for forgiveness of your sins, and therefore for a good conscience before him!

If you are not yet saved, I guarantee you that there are many people praying for you and for your salvation right now! But God cannot answer those prayers against your own free will. The only prayer for YOUR salvation that God can answer is YOURS. Pray it now, as you enter into union with Jesus's death and resurrection in Christian baptism (Colossians 2:12)!

DOXOLOGY
PSALM 19:1-6

The first version of this sermon was preached for Cincinnati Bible Seminary chapel in 1983, then in several churches after that. This final version was preached at the First Church of Christ in Greendale, IN, in 2012.

INTRODUCTION

¹ The heavens declare the glory of God,

and the sky above proclaims his handiwork.

² Day to day pours out speech,

and night to night reveals knowledge.

³ There is no speech, nor are there words,

whose voice is not heard.

⁴ Their voice goes out through all the earth,

and their words to the end of the world.

In them he has set a tent for the sun,

⁵which comes out like a bridegroom leaving his chamber,

and, like a strong man, runs its course with joy.

⁶ Its rising is from the end of the heavens,

and its circuit to the end of them,

and there is nothing hidden from its heat. (ESV)

When I read the words of this Psalm, I think of the term "doxology," and my mind turns to the chorus we often sing in church services:

Praise God from whom all blessings flow!
Praise Him all creatures here below!
Praise Him above, ye heavenly hosts—
Praise Father, Son, and Holy Ghost.

This chorus is actually entitled "Doxology."

What in the world is a doxology? It comes from two Greek words. The "doxo-" part comes from the Greek *doxa*, which is a noun meaning "splendor, majesty, radiance, glory, honor." The "-logy" part is from the Greek *logos*, a familiar word meaning: "word." So a doxology is simply *a word of praise*. This definition fits well with both the Scripture and the chorus quoted above.

Psalms 19 is all about praising and giving glory to God. In 1 Corinthians 10:31 we are commanded thus: "So, whether you eat or drink, or whatever you do, do all to the glory of God." How can we do this? The verses from the Psalm cited above (19:1-6) show us how the universe sets an example of praise. This passage shows us how the heavens and the earth declare the glory of God. We will examine this, and reflect on what our response should be.

I.   THE UNIVERSAL WITNESS TO GOD'S GLORY

The first thing the Psalm says is that the whole creation points to its CREATOR. Verses 1-2 declare, "The heavens declare the glory of God, and the sky above proclaims his handiwork. Day to day pours out speech, and night to night reveals knowledge." This is echoed in Romans 1:20, "For his invisible attributes, namely, his eternal power and divine nature, have been clearly perceived, ever since the creation of the world, in the things that have been made." No matter where you look, the visible voices of nature shout back at you, praising their Maker. Their speech is silent, but universal (vv. 3-4).

The Psalm focuses on "the heavens" and "the sky," and their limitless expanse (v. 1). Just how big is our universe, anyway? The numbers themselves keep expanding as our telescopes get bigger and more efficient, but the latest figures I have seen say that the universe is about 80 billion—that's about 80,000,000,000—light-years across. A light-year is the *distance* light travels in one year. At a speed of about 186,000 miles per *second*, that means that one light-year is about 6 trillion (6,000,000,000.000) miles. Thus the breadth of the observable universe is almost 500 sextillion (500,000,000,000,000,000,000,000) miles—in all directions.

When King David wrote this Psalm (about a thousand years before Christ), no human being would have known this vastness; so the Holy Spirit led David to focus specifically on the way the sun seems to roam across the sky. He describes in poetic language its apparent daily trip between dawn and dusk, as seen by every person on our planet. Even the least sophisticated, most primitive minds on earth can appreciate and enjoy the effects of the sun. But even David did not in his day know the scientific fActs we know today about this wonderful specific creation. Indeed, the more we know about the sun, using techniques of modern science, the greater will be our praise for its Maker!

Here are some recent fActs and figures about the sun. Regarding its size, it is about 865,000 miles in diameter (compared to Earth's c. 8,000 miles); its circumference is about 2,700,000 miles (over 100 times that of the earth); and its surface is 12,000 times that of the Earth. Regarding volume, it is estimated to be 335 quadrillion cubic miles (1,306,000 times that of the Earth); i.e., if the sun were hollow, about 1.3 million Earths would fit inside it! It mass is over 2 billion, billion, billion tons (27 zeroes). Its temperature on the surface is about 10,000 degrees Fahrenheit; at its core it is about 27,000,000 degrees F. Its pressure at the core is estimated to be one billion pounds per square inch. Finally, the sun produces or releases energy at the rate of 380 million, billion, billion (24 more zeroes) watts constantly.

A single solar flare—a leaping tongue of fiery hydrogen sometimes soaring hundreds of thousands of miles above the sun's surface—could provide electrical power for the whole world for one hundred million years. But the earth receives only about one two-billionth of the sun's total energy output—"only" about four million horsepower per square mile of surface.

Now here's the deal: Every inch and every ounce and every degree and every watt of this relatively small star (!) proclaims its Maker's praise! Truly – "The heavens declare the glory of God!" "The unwearied sun from day to day does his Creator's power display – And publishes in every land the work of an almighty hand."

And this is just one small star in a galaxy (the Milky Way) of about 100 billion stars; and the Milky Way is just one of (at today's estimate) between 100 billion and 200 billion total galaxies!

To get an idea of how small our star (the sun) is, let's contrast it with another star in our universe, one called BETELGEUSE, which is located in the constellation Orion, more than six hundred light-years from us. This star is called a red supergiant, and is the eighth brightest star we know. If fact, it is about 14,000 times our sun's brightness. It is also one thousand times larger in diameter than our sun: around 865 million (865,000,000) miles.

To appreciate just how big this is, think of it this way. Imagine that you have superimposed this one star, Betelgeuse, over our entire solar system, with its center and our sun's center being the same. Now imagine that you are in an indestructible spaceship beginning a journey from this center point (the center of Betelgeuse and the center of our sun), moving toward our Earth. You start moving, and first you pass Mercury. Then you pass Venus—and you are still *inside Betelgeuse!* Then you get to the Earth (which is about 93,000,000 miles from our sun)—and you are still *inside Betelgeuse!* Then you keep going, past Mars—and you are still *inside Betelgeuse!* Then you come near Jupiter—and only now do you come to the surface of Betelgeuse! It is about the size of *our entire solar system* out to Jupiter! ONE star!

David did not even know about this when he said, "The heavens declare the glory of God"! No wonder we sing, "Praise Him above, ye heavenly hosts!"

But there's more! This Psalm itself does not go this direction, but the *Earth we live on* also witnesses to God's glory. See Acts 14:17, "Yet he did not leave himself without witness, for he did good by giving you rains from heaven and fruitful seasons, satisfying your hearts with food and gladness." As our Doxology song says, "Praise Him all creatures here below!"

Here I will acknowledge that there is much here upon our planet that causes us to glorify God. Sometimes these witnesses to God's glory are so small that we can see them only through microscopes, but their voices are as loud as that of Betelgeuse the gigantic star!. An example is something I saw on a TV nature show years ago. The show was called "Nature's Defenses." The segment I remember was about a small beetle, the Florida Tortoise beetle (or palmetto tortoise beetle).

This little insect is found in several southern states. It feeds on several southern plants, crawling around on the leaves of these plants. Its main enemy is a species of large ant. When it senses one of these ants approaching, the beetle squats down on its leaf and *clamps its six "feet" down hard on the leaf!* This is where it gets interesting. The little insect has only six feet, but each foot has about 10,000 adhesive bristles, and each bristle has two separate pads. Ordinarily the beetle usually walks "on tiptoe"; but when threatened, all 120,000 pads clamp down and stick to the leaf! At this point each pad secretes an *oily, adhesive substance* that enables the pads to clamp down and stick to the leaf even more securely. The result is that the ant cannot pry the beetle loose; it seems sixty times heavier than it really is—all because of all these pads and their oil, or "toe-jam," or—let's just call it BEETLE JUICE.

You may not be able to see any of these examples I have described here with your normal sight or in your neighborhood, but just look around you wherever your are with your unaided senses: almost everything you experience in nature around you is crying out to the glory of God! – snowflakes, raindrops, lightning, a baby learning to walk, the splendor of a diamond, the songs of birds and whales. What is their message? THE GLORY OF GOD!

What is "glory"? In the New Testament, "glory" is from a word meaning "great, heavy, weighty, important." When used of God it means his infinite excellence, the totality of his perfections, the fullness of his deity. When the heavens and the earth declare the glory of God, they are saying: "Look at us! See what a great Creator we have! The one who made us is infinite in power and majesty! He is GOD!" As another of our hymns says,

> *"This is my Father's world, and to my listening ears*
> *All nature sings, and round me rings the music of the spheres!*
> *This is my Father's world; the birds their carols raise;*
> *The morning light, the lily white, declare their Maker's praise!"*

II. HOW MUST WE RESPOND TO THIS WITNESS TO GOD'S GLORY?

Our next question is this: What shall *we* now do in response to the witness to God's glory that appears all around us? One thing we could do is write a hymn! This is exactly what a 25-year-old Swedish preacher, Carl Boberg, did one day in 1886, after he walked two miles home from church one day in a thunderstorm. Boberg's poetic praise was set later to an old Swedish tune, then translated in 1927 into German, and later still into Russian. Some years later an Englishman, Stuart Hine, heard a Russian translation of what was now used as a hymn, as he was working as a missionary in Czechoslovakia. Later, in 1931 Hine found himself in a mighty thunderstorm in the Carpathian Mountains in Ukraine. The awesome thunder rolling through the mountain range reminded him of the Russian hymn.

Hine began to think of ways to translate this hymn into English. He did so, adding a couple of significant verses of his own. This English version was introduced into the United States at the Billy Graham Crusade in New York City in 1957, especially being sung by Cliff Barrows. The audiences loved it, and that hymn was sung nearly one hundred times in that crusade—and the rest is history.

You know this song. We sing it like this:

> *O Lord my God, when I in awesome wonder*
> *consider all the worlds Thy hands have made;*
> *I see the stars, I hear the rolling thunder—*
> *Thy power throughout the universe displayed!*
> *When through the woods and forest glades I wander*
> *And hear the birds sing sweetly in the trees,*
> *When I look down, from lofty mountain grandeur*
> *And see the brook, and feel the gentle breeze—*
> *Then sings my soul, my Savior God, to Thee:*
> *How great Thou art; how great Thou art!*

The chances of any of us writing a hymn like "How Great Thou Art" are pretty slim. But there is something else we can all do when the glory of the Lord shines round about us in this wonderful world. We can lift up our voices and say – "AMEN!"

Philip Yancey tells of an American writer named Flannery O'Connor, who raised peacocks on her southern farm. She had up to forty at a time; she called them "the king of birds." She once wrote an essay about them, and about the reactions they would get as they unfurled their feathers to present a "galaxy of gazing, haloed suns." One passing truck driver yelled, "Get a load of that!" as he slammed on his brakes. Most people would just stop and stare at them in silence.

But O'Connor's favorite response came from an old African-American woman who, when she saw these strutting birds, simply cried out: "Amen! Amen! Amen!" As Yancey says, "That woman understood praise."

Let's hear an AMEN! for God's wonderful works!

ABOUT THE AUTHOR*

(Photo collage – left to right/top to bottom)

1. Dr. Cottrell's graduation from Princeton Theological Seminary in 1971 with his father, Major. (Yes, his first name was Major.)

2. Jack with his grandsons Zeke and Gabe around 1999. He adores his grandchildren.

3. This bust of Martin Luther was a gift from his wife, Barbara, and on prominent display in Dr. Cottrell's office at the Cincinnati Bible Seminary. As he describes, *"I kind of 'fell in love' with Luther and his theology when I was a student at Westminster Theological Seminary (1962-1965), even though WTS is Calvinist and not Lutheran. The joke was that CBS had a bust of Alexander Campbell in the Grad Study room, but I had a Martin Luther bust."*

4. In 1985, Jack and Barbara Cottrell traveled to Egypt with Professor R. J. Kidwell and his wife, Patsy, to visit Safaa Fahmi of Christian Arabic Services. Jack served on the board of CAS for many years.

5. Jack and Barbara celebrated their 60th anniversary in May 2018!

6. Dr. Cottrell loves to teach – he loves helping people understand the wisdom and blessings of God's word.

---

*Photograph descriptions provided by Cathleen Cottrell.

Made in the USA
Middletown, DE
28 March 2019